MW01288676

The Latin-English Bible – Volume
XVII

PROVERBS
ECCLESIASTES
SONG OF SOLOMON

The texts used in this edition are from the
Vulgate and the King James Version

Compiled by Timothy Plant

Cover picture
The Judgement of Solomon
By
Giorgione

CHAPTER 1

CHAPTER 1

1. parabolae Salomonis filii David regis Israhel
2. ad sciendam sapientiam et disciplinam
3. ad intellegenda verba prudentiae et suscipiendam eruditionem doctrinae iustitiam et iudicium et aequitatem
4. ut detur parvulis astutia adulescenti scientia et intellectus
5. audiens sapiens sapientior erit et intellegens gubernacula possidebit
6. animadvertet parabolam et interpretationem verba sapientium et enigmata eorum
7. timor Domini principium scientiae sapientiam atque doctrinam stulti despiciunt
8. audi fili mi disciplinam patris tui et ne dimittas legem matris tuae

THE proverbs of Solomon the son of David, king of Israel;
2 To know wisdom and instruction; to perceive the words of understanding;
3 To receive the instruction of wisdom, justice, and judgment, and equity;
4 To give subtilty to the simple, to the young man knowledge and discretion.
5 A wise man will hear, and will increase learning; and a man of understanding shall attain unto wise counsels:
6 To understand a proverb, and the interpretation; the words of the wise, and their dark sayings.
7 The fear of the Lord is the beginning of knowledge: but fools despise wisdom and instruction.
8 My son, hear the instruction of thy father, and forsake not the law of thy mother:
9 For they shall be an ornament of grace unto thy

9. ut addatur gratia capiti tuo et torques collo tuo

10. fili mi si te lactaverint peccatores ne adquiescas

11. si dixerint veni nobiscum insidiemur sanguini abscondamus tendiculas contra insontem frustra

12. degluttiamus eum sicut infernus viventem et integrum quasi descendentem in lacum

13. omnem pretiosam substantiam repperiemus implebimus domos nostras spoliis

14. sortem mitte nobiscum marsuppium unum sit omnium nostrum

15. fili mi ne ambules cum eis prohibe pedem tuum a semitis eorum

16. pedes enim illorum ad malum currunt et festinant ut effundant sanguinem

17. frustra autem iacitur rete ante oculos pinnatorum

18. ipsique contra sanguinem suum insidiantur et moliuntur fraudes contra animas suas

head, and chains about thy neck.

10 My son, if sinners entice thee, consent thou not.

11 If they say, Come with us, let us lay wait for blood, let us lurk privily for the innocent without cause:

12 Let us swallow them up alive as the grave; and whole, as those that go down into the pit:

13 We shall find all precious substance, we shall fill our houses with spoil:

14 Cast in thy lot among us; let us all have one purse:

15 My son, walk not thou in the way with them; refrain thy foot from their path:

16 For their feet run to evil, and make haste to shed blood.

17 Surely in vain the net is spread in the sight of any bird.

18 And they lay wait for their own blood; they lurk privily for their own lives.

19 So are the ways of every one that is greedy of gain; which taketh away the life of the owners thereof.

20 Wisdom crieth without; she uttereth her voice in the streets:

19. sic semitae omnis avari animas possidentium rapiunt

20. sapientia foris praedicat in plateis dat vocem suam

21. in capite turbarum clamitat in foribus portarum urbis profert verba sua dicens

22. usquequo parvuli diligitis infantiam et stulti ea quae sibi sunt noxia cupiunt et inprudentes odibunt scientiam

23. convertimini ad correptionem meam en proferam vobis spiritum meum et ostendam verba mea

24. quia vocavi et rennuistis extendi manum meam et non fuit qui aspiceret

25. despexistis omne consilium meum et increpationes meas neglexistis

26. ego quoque in interitu vestro ridebo et subsannabo cum vobis quod timebatis advenerit

27. cum inruerit repentina calamitas et interitus quasi tempestas ingruerit quando venerit super vos

21 She crieth in the chief place of concourse, in the openings of the gates: in the city she uttereth her words, saying,

22 How long, ye simple ones, will ye love simplicity? and the scorners delight in their scorning, and fools hate knowledge?

23 Turn you at my reproof: behold, I will pour out my spirit unto you, I will make known my words unto you.

24 Because I have called, and ye refused; I have stretched out my hand, and no man regarded;

25 But ye have set at nought all my counsel, and would none of my reproof:

26 I also will laugh at your calamity; I will mock when your fear cometh;

27 When your fear cometh as desolation, and your destruction cometh as a whirlwind; when distress and anguish cometh upon you.

28 Then shall they call upon me, but I will not answer; they shall seek me early, but they shall not find me:

29 For that they hated knowledge, and did not choose the fear of the Lord:

tribulatio et angustia

28. tunc invocabunt me et non exaudiam mane consurgent et non invenient me

29. eo quod exosam habuerint disciplinam et timorem Domini non susceperint

30. nec adquieverint consilio meo et detraxerint universae correptioni meae

31. comedent igitur fructus viae suae suisque consiliis saturabuntur

32. aversio parvulorum interficiet eos et prosperitas stultorum perdet illos

33. qui autem me audierit absque terrore requiescet et abundantia perfruetur malorum timore sublato

30 They would none of my counsel: they despised all my reproof.

31 Therefore shall they eat of the fruit of their own way, and be filled with their own devices.

32 For the turning away of the simple shall slay them, and the prosperity of fools shall destroy them.

33 But whoso hearkeneth unto me shall dwell safely, and shall be quiet from fear of evil.

CHAPTER 2

1. fili mi si susceperis sermones meos et mandata mea absconderis penes te

2. ut audiat sapientiam auris tua inclina cor tuum ad noscendam prudentiam

CHAPTER 2

MY son, if thou wilt receive my words, and hide my commandments with thee;

2 So that thou incline thine ear unto wisdom, and apply thine heart to understanding;

3 Yea, if thou criest after knowledge, and liftest up thy

3. si enim sapientiam invocaveris et inclinaveris cor tuum prudentiae

4. si quaesieris eam quasi pecuniam et sicut thesauros effoderis illam

5. tunc intelleges timorem Domini et scientiam Dei invenies

6. quia Dominus dat sapientiam et ex ore eius scientia et prudentia

7. custodiet rectorum salutem et proteget gradientes simpliciter

8. servans semitas iustitiae et vias sanctorum custodiens

9. tunc intelleges iustitiam et iudicium et aequitatem et omnem semitam bonam

10. si intraverit sapientia cor tuum et scientia animae tuae placuerit

11. consilium custodiet te prudentia servabit te

12. ut eruaris de via mala ab homine qui perversa loquitur

13. qui relinquunt iter rectum et ambulant per vias tenebrosas

14. qui laetantur cum malefecerint et exultant

voice for understanding;

4 If thou seekest her as silver, and searchest for her as for hid treasures;

5 Then shalt thou understand the fear of the Lord, and find the knowledge of God.

6 For the Lord giveth wisdom: out of his mouth cometh knowledge and understanding.

7 He layeth up sound wisdom for the righteous: he is a buckler to them that walk uprightly.

8 He keepeth the paths of judgment, and preserveth the way of his saints.

9 Then shalt thou understand righteousness, and judgment, and equity; yea, every good path.

10 When wisdom entereth into thine heart, and knowledge is pleasant unto thy soul;

11 Discretion shall preserve thee, understanding shall keep thee:

12 To deliver thee from the way of the evil man, from the man that speaketh froward things;

13 Who leave the paths of uprightness, to walk in the ways of darkness;

in rebus pessimis
15. quorum viae perversae et infames gressus eorum
16. ut eruaris a muliere aliena et ab extranea quae mollit sermones suos
17. et relinquit ducem pubertatis suae
18. et pacti Dei sui oblita est inclinata est enim ad mortem domus eius et ad impios semitae ipsius
19. omnes qui ingrediuntur ad eam non revertentur nec adprehendent semitas vitae
20. ut ambules in via bona et calles iustorum custodias
21. qui enim recti sunt habitabunt in terra et simplices permanebunt in ea
22. impii vero de terra perdentur et qui inique agunt auferentur ex ea

14 Who rejoice to do evil, and delight in the frowardness of the wicked;
15 Whose ways are crooked, and they froward in their paths:
16 To deliver thee from the strange woman, even from the stranger which flattereth with her words;
17 Which forsaketh the guide of her youth, and forgetteth the covenant of her God.
18 For her house inclineth unto death, and her paths unto the dead.
19 None that go unto her return again, neither take they hold of the paths of life.
20 That thou mayest walk in the way of good men, and keep the paths of the righteous.
21 For the upright shall dwell in the land, and the perfect shall remain in it.
22 But the wicked shall be cut off from the earth, and the transgressors shall be rooted out of it.

1. fili mi ne obliviscaris legis meae et praecepta mea custodiat cor tuum
2. longitudinem enim dierum et annos vitae et pacem adponent tibi
3. misericordia et veritas non te deserant circumda eas gutturi tuo et describe in tabulis cordis tui
4. et invenies gratiam et disciplinam bonam coram Deo et hominibus
5. habe fiduciam in Domino ex toto corde tuo et ne innitaris prudentiae tuae
6. in omnibus viis tuis cogita illum et ipse diriget gressus tuos
7. ne sis sapiens apud temet ipsum time Dominum et recede a malo
8. sanitas quippe erit umbilico tuo et inrigatio ossuum tuorum
9. honora Dominum de tua substantia et de primitiis omnium frugum tuarum
10. et implebuntur horrea tua saturitate et vino

MY son, forget not my law; but let thine heart keep my commandments:

2 For length of days, and long life, and peace, shall they add to thee.

3 Let not mercy and truth forsake thee: bind them about thy neck; write them upon the table of thine heart:

4 So shalt thou find favour and good understanding in the sight of God and man.

5 Trust in the Lord with all thine heart; and lean not unto thine own understanding.

6 In all thy ways acknowledge him, and he shall direct thy paths.

7 Be not wise in thine own eyes: fear the Lord, and depart from evil.

8 It shall be health to thy navel, and marrow to thy bones.

9 Honour the Lord with thy substance, and with the firstfruits of all thine increase:

10 So shall thy barns be filled with plenty, and thy presses shall burst out with new wine.

torcularia redundabunt

11. disciplinam Domini fili mi ne abicias nec deficias cum ab eo corriperis

12. quem enim diligit Dominus corripit et quasi pater in filio conplacet sibi

13. beatus homo qui invenit sapientiam et qui affluit prudentia

14. melior est adquisitio eius negotiatione argenti et auro primo fructus eius

15. pretiosior est cunctis opibus et omnia quae desiderantur huic non valent conparari

16. longitudo dierum in dextera eius in sinistra illius divitiae et gloria

17. viae eius viae pulchrae et omnes semitae illius pacificae

18. lignum vitae est his qui adprehenderint eam et qui tenuerit eam beatus

19. Dominus sapientia fundavit terram stabilivit caelos prudentia

20. sapientia illius eruperunt abyssi et nubes rore concrescunt

21. fili mi ne effluant haec ab oculis tuis

11 My son, despise not the chastening of the Lord; neither be weary of his correction:

12 For whom the Lord loveth he correcteth; even as a father the son in whom he delighteth.

13 Happy is the man that findeth wisdom, and the man that getteth understanding.

14 For the merchandise of it is better than the merchandise of silver, and the gain thereof than fine gold.

15 She is more precious than rubies: and all the things thou canst desire are not to be compared unto her.

16 Length of days is in her right hand; and in her left hand riches and honour.

17 Her ways are ways of pleasantness, and all her paths are peace.

18 She is a tree of life to them that lay hold upon her: and happy is every one that retaineth her.

19 The Lord by wisdom hath founded the earth; by understanding hath he established the heavens.

20 By his knowledge the depths are broken up, and the

custodi legem atque consilium

22. et erit vita animae tuae et gratia faucibus tuis

23. tunc ambulabis fiducialiter in via tua et pes tuus non inpinget

24. si dormieris non timebis quiesces et suavis erit somnus tuus

25. ne paveas repentino terrore et inruentes tibi potentias impiorum

26. Dominus enim erit in latere tuo et custodiet pedem tuum ne capiaris

27. noli prohibere benefacere eum qui potest si vales et ipse benefac

28. ne dicas amico tuo vade et revertere et cras dabo tibi cum statim possis dare

29. ne moliaris amico tuo malum cum ille in te habeat fiduciam

30. ne contendas adversus hominem frustra cum ipse tibi nihil mali fecerit

31. ne aemuleris hominem iniustum nec imiteris vias eius

32. quia abominatio Domini est omnis inlusor

clouds drop down the dew.

21 My son, let not them depart from thine eyes: keep sound wisdom and discretion:

22 So shall they be life unto thy soul, and grace to thy neck.

23 Then shalt thou walk in thy way safely, and thy foot shall not stumble.

24 When thou liest down, thou shalt not be afraid: yea, thou shalt lie down, and thy sleep shall be sweet.

25 Be not afraid of sudden fear, neither of the desolation of the wicked, when it cometh.

26 For the Lord shall be thy confidence, and shall keep thy foot from being taken.

27 Withhold not good from them to whom it is due, when it is in the power of thine hand to do it.

28 Say not unto thy neighbour, Go, and come again, and to morrow I will give; when thou hast it by thee.

29 Devise not evil against thy neighbour, seeing he dwelleth securely by thee.

30 Strive not with a man without cause, if he have

et cum simplicibus sermocinatio eius

33. egestas a Domino in domo impii habitacula autem iustorum benedicentur

34. inlusores ipse deludet et mansuetis dabit gratiam

35. gloriam sapientes possidebunt stultorum exaltatio ignominia

done thee no harm.

31 Envy thou not the oppressor, and choose none of his ways.

32 For the froward is abomination to the Lord: but his secret is with the righteous.

33 The curse of the Lord is in the house of the wicked: but he blesseth the habitation of the just.

34 Surely he scorneth the scorners: but he giveth grace unto the lowly.

35 The wise shall inherit glory: but shame shall be the promotion of fools.

CHAPTER 4

1. audite filii disciplinam patris et adtendite ut sciatis prudentiam

2. donum bonum tribuam vobis legem meam ne derelinquatis

3. nam et ego filius fui patris mei tenellus et unigenitus coram matre mea

4. et docebat me atque dicebat suscipiat verba mea cor tuum custodi praecepta mea et vives

CHAPTER 4

HEAR, ye children, the instruction of a father, and attend to know understanding.

2 For I give you good doctrine, forsake ye not my law.

3 For I was my father's son, tender and only beloved in the sight of my mother.

4 He taught me also, and said unto me, Let thine heart retain my words: keep my commandments, and live.

5. posside sapientiam posside prudentiam ne obliviscaris neque declines a verbis oris mei

6. ne dimittas eam et custodiet te dilige eam et servabit te

7. principium sapientiae posside sapientiam et in omni possessione tua adquire prudentiam

8. arripe illam et exaltabit te glorificaberis ab ea cum eam fueris amplexatus

9. dabit capiti tuo augmenta gratiarum et corona inclita proteget te

10. audi fili mi et suscipe verba mea ut multiplicentur tibi anni vitae

11. viam sapientiae monstravi tibi duxi te per semitas aequitatis

12. quas cum ingressus fueris non artabuntur gressus tui et currens non habebis offendiculum

13. tene disciplinam ne dimittas eam custodi illam quia ipsa est vita tua

14. ne delecteris semitis impiorum nec tibi placeat malorum via

5 Get wisdom, get understanding: forget it not; neither decline from the words of my mouth.

6 Forsake her not, and she shall preserve thee: love her, and she shall keep thee.

7 Wisdom is the principal thing; therefore get wisdom: and with all thy getting get understanding.

8 Exalt her, and she shall promote thee: she shall bring thee to honour, when thou dost embrace her.

9 She shall give to thine head an ornament of grace: a crown of glory shall she deliver to thee.

10 Hear, O my son, and receive my sayings; and the years of thy life shall be many.

11 I have taught thee in the way of wisdom; I have led thee in right paths.

12 When thou goest, thy steps shall not be straitened; and when thou runnest, thou shalt not stumble.

13 Take fast hold of instruction; let her not go: keep her; for she is thy life.

14 Enter not into the path of the wicked, and go not in the way of evil men.

15. fuge ab ea ne transeas per illam declina et desere eam

16. non enim dormiunt nisi malefecerint et rapitur somnus ab eis nisi subplantaverint

17. comedunt panem impietatis et vinum iniquitatis bibunt

18. iustorum autem semita quasi lux splendens procedit et crescit usque ad perfectam diem

19. via impiorum tenebrosa nesciunt ubi corruant

20. fili mi ausculta sermones meos et ad eloquia mea inclina aurem tuam

21. ne recedant ab oculis tuis custodi ea in medio cordis tui

22. vita enim sunt invenientibus ea et universae carni sanitas

23. omni custodia serva cor tuum quia ex ipso vita procedit

24. remove a te os pravum et detrahentia labia sint procul a te

25. oculi tui recta videant et palpebrae tuae

15 Avoid it, pass not by it, turn from it, and pass away.

16 For they sleep not, except they have done mischief; and their sleep is taken away, unless they cause some to fall.

17 For they eat the bread of wickedness, and drink the wine of violence.

18 But the path of the just is as the shining light, that shineth more and more unto the perfect day.

19 The way of the wicked is as darkness: they know not at what they stumble.

20 My son, attend to my words; incline thine ear unto my sayings.

21 Let them not depart from thine eyes; keep them in the midst of thine heart.

22 For they are life unto those that find them, and health to all their flesh.

23 Keep thy heart with all diligence; for out of it are the issues of life.

24 Put away from thee a froward mouth, and perverse lips put far from thee.

25 Let thine eyes look right on, and let thine eyelids look straight before thee.

26 Ponder the path of thy

praecedant gressus tuos
26. dirige semitam pedibus tuis et omnes viae tuae stabilientur
27. ne declines ad dexteram et ad sinistram averte pedem tuum a malo

feet, and let all thy ways be established.
27 Turn not to the right hand nor to the left: remove thy foot from evil.

CHAPTER 5

1. fili mi adtende sapientiam meam et prudentiae meae inclina aurem tuam
2. ut custodias cogitationes et disciplinam labia tua conservent
3. favus enim stillans labia meretricis et nitidius oleo guttur eius
4. novissima autem illius amara quasi absinthium et acuta quasi gladius biceps
5. pedes eius descendunt in mortem et ad inferos gressus illius penetrant
6. per semitam vitae non ambulat vagi sunt gressus eius et investigabiles
7. nunc ergo fili audi me et ne recedas a verbis oris mei

CHAPTER 5

MY son, attend unto my wisdom, and bow thine ear to my understanding:
2 That thou mayest regard discretion, and that thy lips may keep knowledge.
3 For the lips of a strange woman drop as an honeycomb, and her mouth is smoother than oil:
4 But her end is bitter as wormwood, sharp as a twoedged sword.
5 Her feet go down to death; her steps take hold on hell.
6 Lest thou shouldest ponder the path of life, her ways are moveable, that thou canst not know them.
7 Hear me now therefore, O ye children, and depart not from the words of my mouth.
8 Remove thy way far from her, and come not nigh the

8. longe fac ab ea viam tuam et ne adpropinques foribus domus eius

9. ne des alienis honorem tuum et annos tuos crudeli

10. ne forte impleantur extranei viribus tuis et labores tui sint in domo aliena

11. et gemas in novissimis quando consumpseris carnes et corpus tuum et dicas

12. cur detestatus sum disciplinam et increpationibus non adquievit cor meum

13. nec audivi vocem docentium me et magistris non inclinavi aurem meam

14. paene fui in omni malo in medio ecclesiae et synagogae

15. bibe aquam de cisterna tua et fluenta putei tui

16. deriventur fontes tui foras et in plateis aquas tuas divide

17. habeto eas solus nec sint alieni participes tui

18. sit vena tua benedicta et laetare cum muliere adulescentiae tuae

door of her house:

9 Lest thou give thine honour unto others, and thy years unto the cruel:

10 Lest strangers be filled with thy wealth; and thy labours be in the house of a stranger;

11 And thou mourn at the last, when thy flesh and thy body are consumed,

12 And say, How have I hated instruction, and my heart despised reproof;

13 And have not obeyed the voice of my teachers, nor inclined mine ear to them that instructed me!

14 I was almost in all evil in the midst of the congregation and assembly.

15 Drink waters out of thine own cistern, and running waters out of thine own well.

16 Let thy fountains be dispersed abroad, and rivers of waters in the streets.

17 Let them be only thine own, and not strangers' with thee.

18 Let thy fountain be blessed: and rejoice with the wife of thy youth.

19 Let her be as the loving hind and pleasant roe; let her breasts satisfy thee at all

19. cerva carissima et gratissimus hinulus ubera eius inebrient te omni tempore in amore illius delectare iugiter

20. quare seduceris fili mi ab aliena et foveris sinu alterius

21. respicit Dominus vias hominis et omnes gressus illius considerat

22. iniquitates suae capiunt impium et funibus peccatorum suorum constringitur

23. ipse morietur quia non habuit disciplinam et multitudine stultitiae suae decipietur

times; and be thou ravished always with her love.

20 And why wilt thou, my son, be ravished with a strange woman, and embrace the bosom of a stranger?

21 For the ways of man are before the eyes of the Lord, and he pondereth all his goings.

22 His own iniquities shall take the wicked himself, and he shall be holden with the cords of his sins.

23 He shall die without instruction; and in the greatness of his folly he shall go astray.

CHAPTER 6

1. fili mi si spoponderis pro amico tuo defixisti apud extraneum manum tuam

2. inlaqueatus es verbis oris tui et captus propriis sermonibus

3. fac ergo quod dico fili mi et temet ipsum libera quia incidisti in manu proximi tui discurre festina suscita amicum tuum

CHAPTER 6

MY son, if thou be surety for thy friend, if thou hast stricken thy hand with a stranger,

2 Thou art snared with the words of thy mouth, thou art taken with the words of thy mouth.

3 Do this now, my son, and deliver thyself, when thou art come into the hand of thy friend; go, humble thyself, and make sure thy friend.

16

4. ne dederis somnum oculis tuis nec dormitent palpebrae tuae

5. eruere quasi dammula de manu et quasi avis de insidiis aucupis

6. vade ad formicam o piger et considera vias eius et disce sapientiam

7. quae cum non habeat ducem nec praeceptorem nec principem

8. parat aestate cibum sibi et congregat in messe quod comedat

9. usquequo piger dormis quando consurges ex somno tuo

10. paululum dormies paululum dormitabis paululum conseres manus ut dormias

11. et veniet tibi quasi viator egestas et pauperies quasi vir armatus

12. homo apostata vir inutilis graditur ore perverso

13. annuit oculis terit pede digito loquitur

14. pravo corde machinatur malum et in omni tempore iurgia seminat

15. huic extemplo veniet

4 Give not sleep to thine eyes, nor slumber to thine eyelids.

5 Deliver thyself as a roe from the hand of the hunter, and as a bird from the hand of the fowler.

6 Go to the ant, thou sluggard; consider her ways, and be wise:

7 Which having no guide, overseer, or ruler,

8 Provideth her meat in the summer, and gathereth her food in the harvest.

9 How long wilt thou sleep, O sluggard? when wilt thou arise out of thy sleep?

10 Yet a little sleep, a little slumber, a little folding of the hands to sleep:

11 So shall thy poverty come as one that travelleth, and thy want as an armed man.

12 A naughty person, a wicked man, walketh with a froward mouth.

13 He winketh with his eyes, he speaketh with his feet, he teacheth with his fingers;

14 Frowardness is in his heart, he deviseth mischief continually; he soweth discord.

15 Therefore shall his calamity come suddenly;

perditio sua et subito conteretur nec habebit ultra medicinam

16. sex sunt quae odit Dominus et septimum detestatur anima eius

17. oculos sublimes linguam mendacem manus effundentes innoxium sanguinem

18. cor machinans cogitationes pessimas pedes veloces ad currendum in malum

19. proferentem mendacia testem fallacem et eum qui seminat inter fratres discordias

20. conserva fili mi praecepta patris tui et ne dimittas legem matris tuae

21. liga ea in corde tuo iugiter et circumda gutturi tuo

22. cum ambulaveris gradiantur tecum cum dormieris custodiant te et evigilans loquere cum eis

23. quia mandatum lucerna est et lex lux et via vitae increpatio disciplinae

24. ut custodiant te a muliere mala et a blanda lingua extraneae

suddenly shall he be broken without remedy.

16 These six things doth the Lord hate: yea, seven are an abomination unto him:

17 A proud look, a lying tongue, and hands that shed innocent blood,

18 An heart that deviseth wicked imaginations, feet that be swift in running to mischief,

19 A false witness that speaketh lies, and he that soweth discord among brethren.

20 My son, keep thy father's commandment, and forsake not the law of thy mother:

21 Bind them continually upon thine heart, and tie them about thy neck.

22 When thou goest, it shall lead thee; when thou sleepest, it shall keep thee; and when thou awakest, it shall talk with thee.

23 For the commandment is a lamp; and the law is light; and reproofs of instruction are the way of life:

24 To keep thee from the evil woman, from the flattery of the tongue of a strange woman.

25 Lust not after her beauty

25. non concupiscat pulchritudinem eius cor tuum nec capiaris nutibus illius

26. pretium enim scorti vix unius est panis mulier autem viri pretiosam animam capit

27. numquid abscondere potest homo ignem in sinu suo ut vestimenta illius non ardeant

28. aut ambulare super prunas et non conburentur plantae eius

29. sic qui ingreditur ad mulierem proximi sui non erit mundus cum tetigerit eam

30. non grandis est culpae cum quis furatus fuerit furatur enim ut esurientem impleat animam

31. deprehensus quoque reddet septuplum et omnem substantiam domus suae tradet

32. qui autem adulter est propter cordis inopiam perdet animam suam

33. turpitudinem et ignominiam congregat sibi et obprobrium illius non delebitur

34. quia zelus et furor viri

in thine heart; neither let her take thee with her eyelids.

26 For by means of a whorish woman a man is brought to a piece of bread: and the adulteress will hunt for the precious life.

27 Can a man take fire in his bosom, and his clothes not be burned?

28 Can one go upon hot coals, and his feet not be burned?

29 So he that goeth in to his neighbour's wife; whosoever toucheth her shall not be innocent.

30 Men do not despise a thief, if he steal to satisfy his soul when he is hungry;

31 But if he be found, he shall restore sevenfold; he shall give all the substance of his house.

32 But whoso committeth adultery with a woman lacketh understanding: he that doeth it destroyeth his own soul.

33 A wound and dishonour shall he get; and his reproach shall not be wiped away.

34 For jealousy is the rage of a man: therefore he will not spare in the day of vengeance.

non parcet in die vindictae

35. nec adquiescet cuiusquam precibus nec suscipiet pro redemptione dona plurima

35 He will not regard any ransom; neither will he rest content, though thou givest many gifts.

CHAPTER 7

1. fili mi custodi sermones meos et praecepta mea reconde tibi

2. serva mandata mea et vives et legem meam quasi pupillam oculi tui

3. liga eam in digitis tuis scribe illam in tabulis cordis tui

4. dic sapientiae soror mea es et prudentiam voca amicam tuam

5. ut custodiat te a muliere extranea et ab aliena quae verba sua dulcia facit

6. de fenestra enim domus meae per cancellos prospexi

7. et video parvulos considero vecordem iuvenem

8. qui transit in platea iuxta angulum et propter viam domus illius

CHAPTER 7

MY son, keep my words, and lay up my commandments with thee.

2 Keep my commandments, and live; and my law as the apple of thine eye.

3 Bind them upon thy fingers, write them upon the table of thine heart.

4 Say unto wisdom, Thou art my sister; and call understanding thy kinswoman:

5 That they may keep thee from the strange woman, from the stranger which flattereth with her words.

6 For at the window of my house I looked through my casement,

7 And beheld among the simple ones, I discerned among the youths, a young man void of understanding,

8 Passing through the street near her corner; and he went

graditur

9. in obscuro advesperascente die in noctis tenebris et caligine

10. et ecce mulier occurrit illi ornatu meretricio praeparata ad capiendas animas garrula et vaga

11. quietis inpatiens nec valens in domo consistere pedibus suis

12. nunc foris nunc in plateis nunc iuxta angulos insidians

13. adprehensumque deosculatur iuvenem et procaci vultu blanditur dicens

14. victimas pro salute debui hodie reddidi vota mea

15. idcirco egressa sum in occursum tuum desiderans te videre et repperi

16. intexui funibus lectum meum stravi tapetibus pictis ex Aegypto

17. aspersi cubile meum murra et aloe et cinnamomo

18. veni inebriemur uberibus donec inlucescat dies et fruamur cupitis

the way to her house,

9 In the twilight, in the evening, in the black and dark night:

10 And, behold, there met him a woman with the attire of an harlot, and subtil of heart.

11 (She is loud and stubborn; her feet abide not in her house:

12 Now is she without, now in the streets, and lieth in wait at every corner.)

13 So she caught him, and kissed him, and with an impudent face said unto him,

14 I have peace offerings with me; this day have I payed my vows.

15 Therefore came I forth to meet thee, diligently to seek thy face, and I have found thee.

16 I have decked my bed with coverings of tapestry, with carved works, with fine linen of Egypt.

17 I have perfumed my bed with myrrh, aloes, and cinnamon.

18 Come, let us take our fill of love until the morning: let us solace ourselves with loves.

19 For the goodman is not at

amplexibus

19. non est enim vir in domo sua abiit via longissima

20. sacculum pecuniae secum tulit in die plenae lunae reversurus est domum suam

21. inretivit eum multis sermonibus et blanditiis labiorum protraxit illum

22. statim eam sequitur quasi bos ductus ad victimam et quasi agnus lasciviens et ignorans quod ad vincula stultus trahatur

23. donec transfigat sagitta iecur eius velut si avis festinet ad laqueum et nescit quia de periculo animae illius agitur

24. nunc ergo fili audi me et adtende verba oris mei

25. ne abstrahatur in viis illius mens tua neque decipiaris semitis eius

26. multos enim vulneratos deiecit et fortissimi quique interfecti sunt ab ea

27. viae inferi domus eius penetrantes interiora mortis

home, he is gone a long journey:

20 He hath taken a bag of money with him, and will come home at the day appointed.

21 With her much fair speech she caused him to yield, with the flattering of her lips she forced him.

22 He goeth after her straightway, as an ox goeth to the slaughter, or as a fool to the correction of the stocks;

23 Till a dart strike through his liver; as a bird hasteth to the snare, and knoweth not that it is for his life.

24 Hearken unto me now therefore, O ye children, and attend to the words of my mouth.

25 Let not thine heart decline to her ways, go not astray in her paths.

26 For she hath cast down many wounded: yea, many strong men have been slain by her.

27 Her house is the way to hell, going down to the chambers of death.

CHAPTER 8

1. numquid non sapientia clamitat et prudentia dat vocem suam

2. in summis excelsisque verticibus super viam in mediis semitis stans

3. iuxta portas civitatis in ipsis foribus loquitur dicens

4. o viri ad vos clamito et vox mea ad filios hominum

5. intellegite parvuli astutiam et insipientes animadvertite

6. audite quoniam de rebus magnis locutura sum et aperientur labia mea ut recta praedicent

7. veritatem meditabitur guttur meum et labia mea detestabuntur impium

8. iusti sunt omnes sermones mei non est in eis pravum quid neque perversum

9. recti sunt intellegentibus et aequi invenientibus scientiam

10. accipite disciplinam meam et non pecuniam doctrinam magis quam aurum eligite

DOTH not wisdom cry? and understanding put forth her voice?

2 She standeth in the top of high places, by the way in the places of the paths.

3 She crieth at the gates, at the entry of the city, at the coming in at the doors.

4 Unto you, O men, I call; and my voice is to the sons of man.

5 O ye simple, understand wisdom: and, ye fools, be ye of an understanding heart.

6 Hear; for I will speak of excellent things; and the opening of my lips shall be right things.

7 For my mouth shall speak truth; and wickedness is an abomination to my lips.

8 All the words of my mouth are in righteousness; there is nothing froward or perverse in them.

9 They are all plain to him that understandeth, and right to them that find knowledge.

10 Receive my instruction, and not silver; and knowledge rather than choice gold.

11. melior est enim sapientia cunctis pretiosissimis et omne desiderabile ei non potest conparari

12. ego sapientia habito in consilio et eruditis intersum cogitationibus

13. timor Domini odit malum arrogantiam et superbiam et viam pravam et os bilingue detestor

14. meum est consilium et aequitas mea prudentia mea est fortitudo

15. per me reges regnant et legum conditores iusta decernunt

16. per me principes imperant et potentes decernunt iustitiam

17. ego diligentes me diligo et qui mane vigilant ad me invenient me

18. mecum sunt divitiae et gloria opes superbae et iustitia

19. melior est fructus meus auro et pretioso lapide et genimina mea argento electo

20. in viis iustitiae ambulo in medio semitarum iudicii

11 For wisdom is better than rubies; and all the things that may be desired are not to be compared to it.

12 I wisdom dwell with prudence, and find out knowledge of witty inventions.

13 The fear of the Lord is to hate evil: pride, and arrogancy, and the evil way, and the froward mouth, do I hate.

14 Counsel is mine, and sound wisdom: I am understanding; I have strength.

15 By me kings reign, and princes decree justice.

16 By me princes rule, and nobles, even all the judges of the earth.

17 I love them that love me; and those that seek me early shall find me.

18 Riches and honour are with me; yea, durable riches and righteousness.

19 My fruit is better than gold, yea, than fine gold; and my revenue than choice silver.

20 I lead in the way of righteousness, in the midst of the paths of judgment:

21 That I may cause those

21. ut ditem diligentes me et thesauros eorum repleam

22. Dominus possedit me initium viarum suarum antequam quicquam faceret a principio

23. ab aeterno ordita sum et ex antiquis antequam terra fieret

24. necdum erant abyssi et ego iam concepta eram necdum fontes aquarum eruperant

25. necdum montes gravi mole constiterant ante colles ego parturiebar

26. adhuc terram non fecerat et flumina et cardines orbis terrae

27. quando praeparabat caelos aderam quando certa lege et gyro vallabat abyssos

28. quando aethera firmabat sursum et librabat fontes aquarum

29. quando circumdabat mari terminum suum et legem ponebat aquis ne transirent fines suos quando adpendebat fundamenta terrae

30. cum eo eram cuncta conponens et delectabar per singulos dies ludens

that love me to inherit substance; and I will fill their treasures.

22 The Lord possessed me in the beginning of his way, before his works of old.

23 I was set up from everlasting, from the beginning, or ever the earth was.

24 When there were no depths, I was brought forth; when there were no fountains abounding with water.

25 Before the mountains were settled, before the hills was I brought forth:

26 While as yet he had not made the earth, nor the fields, nor the highest part of the dust of the world.

27 When he prepared the heavens, I was there: when he set a compass upon the face of the depth:

28 When he established the clouds above: when he strengthened the fountains of the deep:

29 When he gave to the sea his decree, that the waters should not pass his commandment: when he appointed the foundations of the earth:

30 Then I was by him, as one

coram eo omni tempore
31. ludens in orbe terrarum et deliciae meae esse cum filiis hominum
32. nunc ergo filii audite me beati qui custodiunt vias meas
33. audite disciplinam et estote sapientes et nolite abicere eam
34. beatus homo qui audit me qui vigilat ad fores meas cotidie et observat ad postes ostii mei
35. qui me invenerit inveniet vitam et hauriet salutem a Domino
36. qui autem in me peccaverit laedet animam suam omnes qui me oderunt diligunt mortem

brought up with him: and I was daily his delight, rejoicing always before him;
31 Rejoicing in the habitable part of his earth; and my delights were with the sons of men.
32 Now therefore hearken unto me, O ye children: for blessed are they that keep my ways.
33 Hear instruction, and be wise, and refuse it not.
34 Blessed is the man that heareth me, watching daily at my gates, waiting at the posts of my doors.
35 For whoso findeth me findeth life, and shall obtain favour of the Lord.
36 But he that sinneth against me wrongeth his own soul: all they that hate me love death.

CHAPTER 9

1. sapientia aedificavit sibi domum excidit columnas septem
2. immolavit victimas suas miscuit vinum et proposuit mensam suam
3. misit ancillas suas ut vocarent ad arcem et ad

CHAPTER 9

WISDOM hath builded her house, she hath hewn out her seven pillars:
2 She hath killed her beasts; she hath mingled her wine; she hath also furnished her table.
3 She hath sent forth her

moenia civitatis

4. si quis est parvulus veniat ad me et insipientibus locuta est

5. venite comedite panem meum et bibite vinum quod miscui vobis

6. relinquite infantiam et vivite et ambulate per vias prudentiae

7. qui erudit derisorem ipse sibi facit iniuriam et qui arguit impium generat maculam sibi

8. noli arguere derisorem ne oderit te argue sapientem et diliget te

9. da sapienti et addetur ei sapientia doce iustum et festinabit accipere

10. principium sapientiae timor Domini et scientia sanctorum prudentia

11. per me enim multiplicabuntur dies tui et addentur tibi anni vitae

12. si sapiens fueris tibimet ipsi eris si inlusor solus portabis malum

13. mulier stulta et clamosa plenaque inlecebris et nihil omnino sciens

14. sedit in foribus domus suae super sellam in excelso urbis loco

maidens: she crieth upon the highest places of the city,

4 Whoso is simple, let him turn in hither: as for him that wanteth understanding, she saith to him,

5 Come, eat of my bread, and drink of the wine which I have mingled.

6 Forsake the foolish, and live; and go in the way of understanding.

7 He that reproveth a scorner getteth to himself shame: and he that rebuketh a wicked man getteth himself a blot.

8 Reprove not a scorner, lest he hate thee: rebuke a wise man, and he will love thee.

9 Give instruction to a wise man, and he will be yet wiser: teach a just man, and he will increase in learning.

10 The fear of the Lord is the beginning of wisdom: and the knowledge of the holy is understanding.

11 For by me thy days shall be multiplied, and the years of thy life shall be increased.

12 If thou be wise, thou shalt be wise for thyself: but if thou scornest, thou alone shalt bear it.

13 A foolish woman is clamorous: she is simple, and

15. ut vocaret transeuntes viam et pergentes itinere suo

16. quis est parvulus declinet ad me et vecordi locuta est

17. aquae furtivae dulciores sunt et panis absconditus suavior

18. et ignoravit quod gigantes ibi sint et in profundis inferni convivae eius

knoweth nothing.

14 For she sitteth at the door of her house, on a seat in the high places of the city,

15 To call passengers who go right on their ways:

16 Whoso is simple, let him turn in hither: and as for him that wanteth understanding, she saith to him,

17 Stolen waters are sweet, and bread eaten in secret is pleasant.

18 But he knoweth not that the dead are there; and that her guests are in the depths of hell.

CHAPTER 10

1. parabolae Salomonis filius sapiens laetificat patrem filius vero stultus maestitia est matris suae

2. non proderunt thesauri impietatis iustitia vero liberabit a morte

3. non adfliget Dominus fame animam iusti et insidias impiorum subvertet

4. egestatem operata est manus remissa manus autem fortium divitias parat

CHAPTER 10

THE proverbs of Solomon. A wise son maketh a glad father: but a foolish son is the heaviness of his mother.

2 Treasures of wickedness profit nothing: but righteousness delivereth from death.

3 The Lord will not suffer the soul of the righteous to famish: but he casteth away the substance of the wicked.

4 He becometh poor that dealeth with a slack hand: but the hand of the diligent maketh rich.

5. qui congregat in messe filius sapiens est qui autem stertit aestate filius confusionis

6. benedictio super caput iusti os autem impiorum operit iniquitatem

7. memoria iusti cum laudibus et nomen impiorum putrescet

8. sapiens corde praecepta suscipiet stultus caeditur labiis

9. qui ambulat simpliciter ambulat confidenter qui autem depravat vias suas manifestus erit

10. qui annuit oculo dabit dolorem stultus labiis verberabitur

11. vena vitae os iusti et os impiorum operiet iniquitatem

12. odium suscitat rixas et universa delicta operit caritas

13. in labiis sapientis invenietur sapientia et virga in dorso eius qui indiget corde

14. sapientes abscondunt scientiam os autem stulti confusioni proximum est

15. substantia divitis urbs fortitudinis eius pavor pauperum egestas eorum

5 He that gathereth in summer is a wise son: but he that sleepeth in harvest is a son that causeth shame.

6 Blessings are upon the head of the just: but violence covereth the mouth of the wicked.

7 The memory of the just is blessed: but the name of the wicked shall rot.

8 The wise in heart will receive commandments: but a prating fool shall fall.

9 He that walketh uprightly walketh surely: but he that perverteth his ways shall be known.

10 He that winketh with the eye causeth sorrow: but a prating fool shall fall.

11 The mouth of a righteous man is a well of life: but violence covereth the mouth of the wicked.

12 Hatred stirreth up strifes: but love covereth all sins.

13 In the lips of him that hath understanding wisdom is found: but a rod is for the back of him that is void of understanding.

14 Wise men lay up knowledge: but the mouth of the foolish is near destruction.

16. opus iusti ad vitam fructus impii ad peccatum
17. via vitae custodienti disciplinam qui autem increpationes relinquit errat
18. abscondunt odium labia mendacia qui profert contumeliam insipiens est
19. in multiloquio peccatum non deerit qui autem moderatur labia sua prudentissimus est
20. argentum electum lingua iusti cor impiorum pro nihilo
21. labia iusti erudiunt plurimos qui autem indocti sunt in cordis egestate morientur
22. benedictio Domini divites facit nec sociabitur ei adflictio
23. quasi per risum stultus operatur scelus sapientia autem est viro prudentia
24. quod timet impius veniet super eum desiderium suum iustis dabitur
25. quasi tempestas transiens non erit impius iustus autem quasi fundamentum

15 The rich man's wealth is his strong city: the destruction of the poor is their poverty.
16 The labour of the righteous tendeth to life: the fruit of the wicked to sin.
17 He is in the way of life that keepeth instruction: but he that refuseth reproof erreth.
18 He that hideth hatred with lying lips, and he that uttereth a slander, is a fool.
19 In the multitude of words there wanteth not sin: but he that refraineth his lips is wise.
20 The tongue of the just is as choice silver: the heart of the wicked is little worth.
21 The lips of the righteous feed many: but fools die for want of wisdom.
22 The blessing of the Lord, it maketh rich, and he addeth no sorrow with it.
23 It is as sport to a fool to do mischief: but a man of understanding hath wisdom.
24 The fear of the wicked, it shall come upon him: but the desire of the righteous shall be granted.
25 As the whirlwind passeth, so is the wicked no more: but

sempiternum

26. sicut acetum dentibus et fumus oculis sic piger his qui miserunt eum

27. timor Domini adponet dies et anni impiorum breviabuntur

28. expectatio iustorum laetitia spes autem impiorum peribit

29. fortitudo simplicis via Domini et pavor his qui operantur malum

30. iustus in aeternum non commovebitur impii autem non habitabunt in terram

31. os iusti parturiet sapientiam lingua pravorum peribit

32. labia iusti considerant placita et os impiorum perversa

the righteous is an everlasting foundation.

26 As vinegar to the teeth, and as smoke to the eyes, so is the sluggard to them that send him.

27 The fear of the Lord prolongeth days: but the years of the wicked shall be shortened.

28 The hope of the righteous shall be gladness: but the expectation of the wicked shall perish.

29 The way of the Lord is strength to the upright: but destruction shall be to the workers of iniquity.

30 The righteous shall never be removed: but the wicked shall not inhabit the earth.

31 The mouth of the just bringeth forth wisdom: but the froward tongue shall be cut out.

32 The lips of the righteous know what is acceptable: but the mouth of the wicked speaketh frowardness.

CHAPTER 11

CHAPTER 11

1. statera dolosa abominatio apud Dominum et pondus

A FALSE balance is abomination to the Lord: but a just weight is his delight.

aequum voluntas eius

2. ubi fuerit superbia ibi erit et contumelia ubi autem humilitas ibi et sapientia

3. simplicitas iustorum diriget eos et subplantatio perversorum vastabit illos

4. non proderunt divitiae in die ultionis iustitia autem liberabit a morte

5. iustitia simplicis diriget viam eius et in impietate sua corruet impius

6. iustitia rectorum liberabit eos et in insidiis suis capientur iniqui

7. mortuo homine impio nulla erit ultra spes et expectatio sollicitorum peribit

8. iustus de angustia liberatus est et tradetur impius pro eo

9. simulator ore decipit amicum suum iusti autem liberabuntur scientia

10. in bonis iustorum exultabit civitas et in perditione impiorum erit laudatio

11. benedictione iustorum exaltabitur civitas et ore impiorum subvertetur

12. qui despicit amicum suum indigens corde est

2 When pride cometh, then cometh shame: but with the lowly is wisdom.

3 The integrity of the upright shall guide them: but the perverseness of transgressors shall destroy them.

4 Riches profit not in the day of wrath: but righteousness delivereth from death.

5 The righteousness of the perfect shall direct his way: but the wicked shall fall by his own wickedness.

6 The righteousness of the upright shall deliver them: but transgressors shall be taken in their own naughtiness.

7 When a wicked man dieth, his expectation shall perish: and the hope of unjust men perisheth.

8 The righteous is delivered out of trouble, and the wicked cometh in his stead.

9 An hypocrite with his mouth destroyeth his neighbour: but through knowledge shall the just be delivered.

10 When it goeth well with the righteous, the city rejoiceth: and when the wicked perish, there is shouting.

vir autem prudens tacebit
13. qui ambulat fraudulenter revelat arcana qui autem fidelis est animi celat commissum
14. ubi non est gubernator populus corruet salus autem ubi multa consilia
15. adfligetur malo qui fidem facit pro extraneo qui autem cavet laqueos securus erit
16. mulier gratiosa inveniet gloriam et robusti habebunt divitias
17. benefacit animae suae vir misericors qui autem crudelis est et propinquos abicit
18. impius facit opus instabile seminanti autem iustitiam merces fidelis
19. clementia praeparat vitam et sectatio malorum mortem
20. abominabile Domino pravum cor et voluntas eius in his qui simpliciter ambulant
21. manus in manu non erit innocens malus semen autem iustorum salvabitur
22. circulus aureus in

11 By the blessing of the upright the city is exalted: but it is overthrown by the mouth of the wicked.

12 He that is void of wisdom despiseth his neighbour: but a man of understanding holdeth his peace.

13 A talebearer revealeth secrets: but he that is of a faithful spirit concealeth the matter.

14 Where no counsel is, the people fall: but in the multitude of counsellers there is safety.

15 He that is surety for a stranger shall smart for it: and he that hateth suretiship is sure.

16 A gracious woman retaineth honour: and strong men retain riches.

17 The merciful man doeth good to his own soul: but he that is cruel troubleth his own flesh.

18 The wicked worketh a deceitful work: but to him that soweth righteousness shall be a sure reward.

19 As righteousness tendeth to life: so he that pursueth evil pursueth it to his own death.

20 They that are of a froward

naribus suis mulier pulchra et fatua

23. desiderium iustorum omne bonum est praestolatio impiorum furor

24. alii dividunt propria et ditiores fiunt alii rapiunt non sua et semper in egestate sunt

25. anima quae benedicit inpinguabitur et qui inebriat ipse quoque inebriabitur

26. qui abscondit frumenta maledicetur in populis benedictio autem super caput vendentium

27. bene consurgit diluculo qui quaerit bona qui autem investigator malorum est opprimetur ab eis

28. qui confidet in divitiis suis corruet iusti autem quasi virens folium germinabunt

29. qui conturbat domum suam possidebit ventos et qui stultus est serviet sapienti

30. fructus iusti lignum vitae et qui suscipit animas sapiens est

31. si iustus in terra recipit quanto magis

heart are abomination to the Lord: but such as are upright in their way are his delight.

21 Though hand join in hand, the wicked shall not be unpunished: but the seed of the righteous shall be delivered.

22 As a jewel of gold in a swine's snout, so is a fair woman which is without discretion.

23 The desire of the righteous is only good: but the expectation of the wicked is wrath.

24 There is that scattereth, and yet increaseth; and there is that withholdeth more than is meet, but it tendeth to poverty.

25 The liberal soul shall be made fat: and he that watereth shall be watered also himself.

26 He that withholdeth corn, the people shall curse him: but blessing shall be upon the head of him that selleth it.

27 He that diligently seeketh good procureth favour: but he that seeketh mischief, it shall come unto him.

28 He that trusteth in his riches shall fall: but the righteous shall flourish as a

impius et peccator

branch.

29 He that troubleth his own house shall inherit the wind: and the fool shall be servant to the wise of heart.

30 The fruit of the righteous is a tree of life; and he that winneth souls is wise.

31 Behold, the righteous shall be recompensed in the earth: much more the wicked and the sinner.

CHAPTER 12

CHAPTER 12

1. qui diligit disciplinam diligit scientiam qui autem odit increpationes insipiens est

2. qui bonus est hauriet a Domino gratiam qui autem confidit cogitationibus suis impie agit

3. non roborabitur homo ex impietate et radix iustorum non commovebitur

4. mulier diligens corona viro suo et putredo in ossibus eius quae confusione res dignas gerit

5. cogitationes iustorum iudicia et consilia

WHOSO loveth instruction loveth knowledge: but he that hateth reproof is brutish.

2 A good man obtaineth favour of the Lord: but a man of wicked devices will he condemn.

3 A man shall not be established by wickedness: but the root of the righteous shall not be moved.

4 A virtuous woman is a crown to her husband: but she that maketh ashamed is as rottenness in his bones.

5 The thoughts of the righteous are right: but the counsels of the wicked are deceit.

6 The words of the wicked

impiorum fraudulentia

6. verba impiorum insidiantur sanguini os iustorum liberabit eos

7. verte impios et non erunt domus autem iustorum permanebit

8. doctrina sua noscetur vir qui autem vanus et excors est patebit contemptui

9. melior est pauper et sufficiens sibi quam gloriosus et indigens pane

10. novit iustus animas iumentorum suorum viscera autem impiorum crudelia

11. qui operatur terram suam saturabitur panibus qui autem sectatur otium stultissimus est

12. desiderium impii munimentum est pessimorum radix autem iustorum proficiet

13. propter peccata labiorum ruina proximat malo effugiet autem iustus de angustia

14. de fructu oris sui unusquisque replebitur bonis et iuxta opera manuum suarum retribuetur ei

15. via stulti recta in

are to lie in wait for blood: but the mouth of the upright shall deliver them.

7 The wicked are overthrown, and are not: but the house of the righteous shall stand.

8 A man shall be commended according to his wisdom: but he that is of a perverse heart shall be despised.

9 He that is despised, and hath a servant, is better than he that honoureth himself, and lacketh bread.

10 A righteous man regardeth the life of his beast: but the tender mercies of the wicked are cruel.

11 He that tilleth his land shall be satisfied with bread: but he that followeth vain persons is void of understanding.

12 The wicked desireth the net of evil men: but the root of the righteous yieldeth fruit.

13 The wicked is snared by the transgression of his lips: but the just shall come out of trouble.

14 A man shall be satisfied with good by the fruit of his mouth: and the recompence

oculis eius qui autem sapiens est audit consilia

16. fatuus statim indicat iram suam qui autem dissimulat iniuriam callidus est

17. qui quod novit loquitur index iustitiae est qui autem mentitur testis est fraudulentus

18. est qui promittit et quasi gladio pungitur conscientiae lingua autem sapientium sanitas est

19. labium veritatis firmum erit in perpetuum qui autem testis est repentinus concinnat linguam mendacii

20. dolus in corde cogitantium mala qui autem ineunt pacis consilia sequitur eos gaudium

21. non contristabit iustum quicquid ei acciderit impii autem replebuntur malo

22. abominatio Domino labia mendacia qui autem fideliter agunt placent ei

23. homo versutus celat scientiam et cor insipientium provocabit stultitiam

24. manus fortium

of a man's hands shall be rendered unto him.

15 The way of a fool is right in his own eyes: but he that hearkeneth unto counsel is wise.

16 A fool's wrath is presently known: but a prudent man covereth shame.

17 He that speaketh truth sheweth forth righteousness: but a false witness deceit.

18 There is that speaketh like the piercings of a sword: but the tongue of the wise is health.

19 The lip of truth shall be established for ever: but a lying tongue is but for a moment.

20 Deceit is in the heart of them that imagine evil: but to the counsellers of peace is joy.

21 There shall no evil happen to the just: but the wicked shall be filled with mischief.

22 Lying lips are abomination to the Lord: but they that deal truly are his delight.

23 A prudent man concealeth knowledge: but the heart of fools proclaimeth foolishness.

24 The hand of the diligent

dominabitur quae autem remissa est tributis serviet 25. maeror in corde viri humiliabit illud et sermone bono laetificabitur

26. qui neglegit damnum propter amicum iustus est iter autem impiorum decipiet eos

27. non inveniet fraudulentus lucrum et substantia hominis erit auri pretium

28. in semita iustitiae vita iter autem devium ducit ad mortem

shall bear rule: but the slothful shall be under tribute.

25 Heaviness in the heart of man maketh it stoop: but a good word maketh it glad.

26 The righteous is more excellent than his neighbour: but the way of the wicked seduceth them.

27 The slothful man roasteth not that which he took in hunting: but the substance of a diligent man is precious.

28 In the way of righteousness is life; and in the pathway thereof there is no death.

CHAPTER 13

CHAPTER 13

1. filius sapiens doctrina patris qui autem inlusor est non audit cum arguitur

2. de fructu oris homo saturabitur bonis anima autem praevaricatorum iniqua

3. qui custodit os suum custodit animam suam qui autem inconsideratus est ad loquendum sentiet mala

4. vult et non vult piger

A WISE son heareth his father's instruction: but a scorner heareth not rebuke.

2 A man shall eat good by the fruit of his mouth: but the soul of the transgressors shall eat violence.

3 He that keepeth his mouth keepeth his life: but he that openeth wide his lips shall have destruction.

4 The soul of the sluggard desireth, and hath nothing: but the soul of the diligent

anima autem operantium inpinguabitur

5. verbum mendax iustus detestabitur impius confundit et confundetur

6. iustitia custodit innocentis viam impietas vero peccato subplantat

7. est quasi dives cum nihil habeat et est quasi pauper cum in multis divitiis sit

8. redemptio animae viri divitiae suae qui autem pauper est increpationem non sustinet

9. lux iustorum laetificat lucerna autem impiorum extinguetur

10. inter superbos semper iurgia sunt qui autem agunt cuncta consilio reguntur sapientia

11. substantia festinata minuetur quae autem paulatim colligitur manu multiplicabitur

12. spes quae differtur adfligit animam lignum vitae desiderium veniens

13. qui detrahit alicui rei ipse se in futurum obligat qui autem timet praeceptum in pace versabitur

14. lex sapientis fons

shall be made fat.

5 A righteous man hateth lying: but a wicked man is loathsome, and cometh to shame.

6 Righteousness keepeth him that is upright in the way: but wickedness overthroweth the sinner.

7 There is that maketh himself rich, yet hath nothing: there is that maketh himself poor, yet hath great riches.

8 The ransom of a man's life are his riches: but the poor heareth not rebuke.

9 The light of the righteous rejoiceth: but the lamp of the wicked shall be put out.

10 Only by pride cometh contention: but with the well advised is wisdom.

11 Wealth gotten by vanity shall be diminished: but he that gathereth by labour shall increase.

12 Hope deferred maketh the heart sick: but when the desire cometh, it is a tree of life.

13 Whoso despiseth the word shall be destroyed: but he that feareth the commandment shall be rewarded.

vitae ut declinet a ruina mortis

15. doctrina bona dabit gratiam in itinere contemptorum vorago

16. astutus omnia agit cum consilio qui autem fatuus est aperit stultitiam

17. nuntius impii cadet in malum legatus fidelis sanitas

18. egestas et ignominia ei qui deserit disciplinam qui autem adquiescit arguenti glorificabitur

19. desiderium si conpleatur delectat animam detestantur stulti eos qui fugiunt mala

20. qui cum sapientibus graditur sapiens erit amicus stultorum efficietur similis

21. peccatores persequetur malum et iustis retribuentur bona

22. bonus relinquet heredes filios et nepotes et custoditur iusto substantia peccatoris

23. multi cibi in novalibus patrum et alii congregantur absque iudicio

24. qui parcit virgae suae odit filium suum qui

14 The law of the wise is a fountain of life, to depart from the snares of death.

15 Good understanding giveth favour: but the way of transgressors is hard.

16 Every prudent man dealeth with knowledge: but a fool layeth open his folly.

17 A wicked messenger falleth into mischief: but a faithful ambassador is health.

18 Poverty and shame shall be to him that refuseth instruction: but he that regardeth reproof shall be honoured.

19 The desire accomplished is sweet to the soul: but it is abomination to fools to depart from evil.

20 He that walketh with wise men shall be wise: but a companion of fools shall be destroyed.

21 Evil pursueth sinners: but to the righteous good shall be repayed.

22 A good man leaveth an inheritance to his children's children: and the wealth of the sinner is laid up for the just.

23 Much food is in the tillage of the poor: but there is that is destroyed for want of

autem diligit illum instanter erudit

25. iustus comedit et replet animam suam venter autem impiorum insaturabilis

judgment.

24 He that spareth his rod hateth his son: but he that loveth him chasteneth him betimes.

25 The righteous eateth to the satisfying of his soul: but the belly of the wicked shall want.

CHAPTER 14

CHAPTER 14

1. sapiens mulier aedificavit domum suam insipiens instructam quoque destruet manibus

2. ambulans recto itinere et timens Deum despicitur ab eo qui infami graditur via

3. in ore stulti virga superbiae labia sapientium custodiunt eos

4. ubi non sunt boves praesepe vacuum est ubi autem plurimae segetes ibi manifesta fortitudo bovis

5. testis fidelis non mentietur profert mendacium testis dolosus

6. quaerit derisor sapientiam et non inveniet doctrina prudentium facilis

EVERY wise woman buildeth her house: but the foolish plucketh it down with her hands.

2 He that walketh in his uprightness feareth the Lord: but he that is perverse in his ways despiseth him.

3 In the mouth of the foolish is a rod of pride: but the lips of the wise shall preserve them.

4 Where no oxen are, the crib is clean: but much increase is by the strength of the ox.

5 A faithful witness will not lie: but a false witness will utter lies.

6 A scorner seeketh wisdom, and findeth it not: but knowledge is easy unto him that understandeth.

7 Go from the presence of a

7. vade contra virum stultum et nescito labia prudentiae

8. sapientia callidi est intellegere viam suam et inprudentia stultorum errans

9. stultis inludet peccatum inter iustos morabitur gratia

10. cor quod novit amaritudinem animae suae in gaudio eius non miscebitur extraneus

11. domus impiorum delebitur tabernacula iustorum germinabunt

12. est via quae videtur homini iusta novissima autem eius deducunt ad mortem

13. risus dolore miscebitur et extrema gaudii luctus occupat

14. viis suis replebitur stultus et super eum erit vir bonus

15. innocens credit omni verbo astutus considerat gressus suos

16. sapiens timet et declinat malum stultus transilit et confidit

17. inpatiens operabitur stultitiam et vir versutus odiosus est

foolish man, when thou perceivest not in him the lips of knowledge.

8 The wisdom of the prudent is to understand his way: but the folly of fools is deceit.

9 Fools make a mock at sin: but among the righteous there is favour.

10 The heart knoweth his own bitterness; and a stranger doth not intermeddle with his joy.

11 The house of the wicked shall be overthrown: but the tabernacle of the upright shall flourish.

12 There is a way which seemeth right unto a man, but the end thereof are the ways of death.

13 Even in laughter the heart is sorrowful; and the end of that mirth is heaviness.

14 The backslider in heart shall be filled with his own ways: and a good man shall be satisfied from himself.

15 The simple believeth every word: but the prudent man looketh well to his going.

16 A wise man feareth, and departeth from evil: but the fool rageth, and is confident.

17 He that is soon angry

18. possidebunt parvuli stultitiam et astuti expectabunt scientiam

19. iacebunt mali ante bonos et impii ante portas iustorum

20. etiam proximo suo pauper odiosus erit amici vero divitum multi

21. qui despicit proximum suum peccat qui autem miseretur pauperi beatus erit

22. errant qui operantur malum misericordia et veritas praeparant bona

23. in omni opere erit abundantia ubi autem verba sunt plurima frequenter egestas

24. corona sapientium divitiae eorum fatuitas stultorum inprudentia

25. liberat animas testis fidelis et profert mendacia versipellis

26. in timore Domini fiducia fortitudinis et filiis eius erit spes

27. timor Domini fons vitae ut declinet a ruina mortis

28. in multitudine populi dignitas regis et in paucitate plebis ignominia principis

dealeth foolishly: and a man of wicked devices is hated.

18 The simple inherit folly: but the prudent are crowned with knowledge.

19 The evil bow before the good; and the wicked at the gates of the righteous.

20 The poor is hated even of his own neighbour: but the rich hath many friends.

21 He that despiseth his neighbour sinneth: but he that hath mercy on the poor, happy is he.

22 Do they not err that devise evil? but mercy and truth shall be to them that devise good.

23 In all labour there is profit: but the talk of the lips tendeth only to penury.

24 The crown of the wise is their riches: but the foolishness of fools is folly.

25 A true witness delivereth souls: but a deceitful witness speaketh lies.

26 In the fear of the Lord is strong confidence: and his children shall have a place of refuge.

27 The fear of the Lord is a fountain of life, to depart from the snares of death.

28 In the multitude of people

29. qui patiens est multa gubernatur prudentia qui autem inpatiens exaltat stultitiam suam

30. vita carnium sanitas cordis putredo ossuum invidia

31. qui calumniatur egentem exprobrat factori eius honorat autem eum qui miseretur pauperis

32. in malitia sua expelletur impius sperat autem iustus in morte sua

33. in corde prudentis requiescit sapientia et indoctos quoque erudiet

34. iustitia elevat gentem miseros facit populos peccatum

35. acceptus est regi minister intellegens iracundiam eius inutilis sustinebit

is the king's honour: but in the want of people is the destruction of the prince.

29 He that is slow to wrath is of great understanding: but he that is hasty of spirit exalteth folly.

30 A sound heart is the life of the flesh: but envy the rottenness of the bones.

31 He that oppresseth the poor reproacheth his Maker: but he that honoureth him hath mercy on the poor.

32 The wicked is driven away in his wickedness: but the righteous hath hope in his death.

33 Wisdom resteth in the heart of him that hath understanding: but that which is in the midst of fools is made known.

34 Righteousness exalteth a nation: but sin is a reproach to any people.

35 The king's favour is toward a wise servant: but his wrath is against him that causeth shame.

1. responsio mollis frangit iram sermo durus suscitat furorem

2. lingua sapientium ornat scientiam os fatuorum ebullit stultitiam

3. in omni loco oculi Domini contemplantur malos et bonos

4. lingua placabilis lignum vitae quae inmoderata est conteret spiritum

5. stultus inridet disciplinam patris sui qui autem custodit increpationes astutior fiet

6. domus iusti plurima fortitudo et in fructibus impii conturbatur

7. labia sapientium disseminabunt scientiam cor stultorum dissimile erit

8. victimae impiorum abominabiles Domino vota iustorum placabilia

9. abominatio est Domino via impii qui sequitur iustitiam diligetur ab eo

10. doctrina mala deserenti viam qui increpationes odit

A SOFT answer turneth away wrath: but grievous words stir up anger.

2 The tongue of the wise useth knowledge aright: but the mouth of fools poureth out foolishness.

3 The eyes of the Lord are in every place, beholding the evil and the good.

4 A wholesome tongue is a tree of life: but perverseness therein is a breach in the spirit.

5 A fool despiseth his father's instruction: but he that regardeth reproof is prudent.

6 In the house of the righteous is much treasure: but in the revenues of the wicked is trouble.

7 The lips of the wise disperse knowledge: but the heart of the foolish doeth not so.

8 The sacrifice of the wicked is an abomination to the Lord: but the prayer of the upright is his delight.

9 The way of the wicked is an abomination unto the Lord: but he loveth him that

morietur

11. infernus et perditio coram Domino quanto magis corda filiorum hominum

12. non amat pestilens eum qui se corripit nec ad sapientes graditur

13. cor gaudens exhilarat faciem in maerore animi deicitur spiritus

14. cor sapientis quaerit doctrinam et os stultorum pascetur inperitia

15. omnes dies pauperis mali secura mens quasi iuge convivium

16. melius est parum cum timore Domini quam thesauri magni et insatiabiles

17. melius est vocare ad holera cum caritate quam ad vitulum saginatum cum odio

18. vir iracundus provocat rixas qui patiens est mitigat suscitatas

19. iter pigrorum quasi sepes spinarum via iustorum absque offendiculo

20. filius sapiens laetificat patrem et stultus homo despicit matrem suam

followeth after righteousness.

10 Correction is grievous unto him that forsaketh the way: and he that hateth reproof shall die.

11 Hell and destruction are before the Lord: how much more then the hearts of the children of men?

12 A scorner loveth not one that reproveth him: neither will he go unto the wise.

13 A merry heart maketh a cheerful countenance: but by sorrow of the heart the spirit is broken.

14 The heart of him that hath understanding seeketh knowledge: but the mouth of fools feedeth on foolishness.

15 All the days of the afflicted are evil: but he that is of a merry heart hath a continual feast.

16 Better is little with the fear of the Lord than great treasure and trouble therewith.

17 Better is a dinner of herbs where love is, than a stalled ox and hatred therewith.

18 A wrathful man stirreth up strife: but he that is slow to anger appeaseth strife.

19 The way of the slothful man is as an hedge of thorns:

21. stultitia gaudium stulto et vir prudens dirigit gressus

22. dissipantur cogitationes ubi non est consilium ubi vero plures sunt consiliarii confirmantur

23. laetatur homo in sententia oris sui et sermo oportunus est optimus

24. semita vitae super eruditum ut declinet de inferno novissimo

25. domum superborum demolietur Dominus et firmos facit terminos viduae

26. abominatio Domini cogitationes malae et purus sermo pulcherrimus

27. conturbat domum suam qui sectatur avaritiam qui autem odit munera vivet

28. mens iusti meditatur oboedientiam os impiorum redundat malis

29. longe est Dominus ab impiis et orationes iustorum exaudiet

30. lux oculorum laetificat animam fama bona inpinguat ossa

31. auris quae audit increpationes vitae in

but the way of the righteous is made plain.

20 A wise son maketh a glad father: but a foolish man despiseth his mother.

21 Folly is joy to him that is destitute of wisdom: but a man of understanding walketh uprightly.

22 Without counsel purposes are disappointed: but in the multitude of counsellers they are established.

23 A man hath joy by the answer of his mouth: and a word spoken in due season, how good is it!

24 The way of life is above to the wise, that he may depart from hell beneath.

25 The Lord will destroy the house of the proud: but he will establish the border of the widow.

26 The thoughts of the wicked are an abomination to the Lord: but the words of the pure are pleasant words.

27 He that is greedy of gain troubleth his own house; but he that hateth gifts shall live.

28 The heart of the righteous studieth to answer: but the mouth of the wicked poureth out evil things.

29 The Lord is far from the

medio sapientium commorabitur

32. qui abicit disciplinam despicit animam suam qui adquiescit increpationibus possessor est cordis

33. timor Domini disciplina sapientiae et gloriam praecedit humilitas

wicked: but he heareth the prayer of the righteous.

30 The light of the eyes rejoiceth the heart: and a good report maketh the bones fat.

31 The ear that heareth the reproof of life abideth among the wise.

32 He that refuseth instruction despiseth his own soul: but he that heareth reproof getteth understanding.

33 The fear of the Lord is the instruction of wisdom; and before honour is humility.

CHAPTER 16

1. hominis est animum praeparare et Dei gubernare linguam

2. omnes viae hominum patent oculis eius spirituum ponderator est Dominus

3. revela Domino opera tua et dirigentur cogitationes tuae

4. universa propter semet ipsum operatus est Dominus impium quoque ad diem malum

5. abominatio Domini

CHAPTER 16

THE preparations of the heart in man, and the answer of the tongue, is from the Lord.

2 All the ways of a man are clean in his own eyes; but the Lord weigheth the spirits.

3 Commit thy works unto the Lord, and thy thoughts shall be established.

4 The Lord hath made all things for himself: yea, even the wicked for the day of evil.

5 Every one that is proud in

omnis arrogans etiam si manus ad manum fuerit non erit innocens

6. misericordia et veritate redimitur iniquitas et in timore Domini declinatur a malo

7. cum placuerint Domino viae hominis inimicos quoque eius convertet ad pacem

8. melius est parum cum iustitia quam multi fructus cum iniquitate

9. cor hominis disponet viam suam sed Domini est dirigere gressus eius

10. divinatio in labiis regis in iudicio non errabit os eius

11. pondus et statera iudicia Domini sunt et opera eius omnes lapides sacculi

12. abominabiles regi qui agunt impie quoniam iustitia firmatur solium

13. voluntas regum labia iusta qui recta loquitur diligetur

14. indignatio regis nuntii mortis et vir sapiens placabit eam

15. in hilaritate vultus regis vita et clementia eius quasi imber serotinus

heart is an abomination to the Lord: though hand join in hand, he shall not be unpunished.

6 By mercy and truth iniquity is purged: and by the fear of the Lord men depart from evil.

7 When a man's ways please the Lord, he maketh even his enemies to be at peace with him.

8 Better is a little with righteousness than great revenues without right.

9 A man's heart deviseth his way: but the Lord directeth his steps.

10 A divine sentence is in the lips of the king: his mouth transgresseth not in judgment.

11 A just weight and balance are the Lord's: all the weights of the bag are his work.

12 It is an abomination to kings to commit wickedness: for the throne is established by righteousness.

13 Righteous lips are the delight of kings; and they love him that speaketh right.

14 The wrath of a king is as messengers of death: but a wise man will pacify it.

16. posside sapientiam quia auro melior est et adquire prudentiam quia pretiosior est argento

17. semita iustorum declinat mala custos animae suae servat viam suam

18. contritionem praecedit superbia et ante ruinam exaltatur spiritus

19. melius est humiliari cum mitibus quam dividere spolia cum superbis

20. eruditus in verbo repperiet bona et qui in Domino sperat beatus est

21. qui sapiens corde est appellabitur prudens et qui dulcis eloquio maiora percipiet

22. fons vitae eruditio possidentis doctrina stultorum fatuitas

23. cor sapientis erudiet os eius et labiis illius addet gratiam

24. favus mellis verba conposita dulcedo animae et sanitas ossuum

25. est via quae videtur homini recta et novissimum eius ducit ad mortem

26. anima laborantis

15 In the light of the king's countenance is life; and his favour is as a cloud of the latter rain.

16 How much better is it to get wisdom than gold! and to get understanding rather to be chosen than silver!

17 The highway of the upright is to depart from evil: he that keepeth his way preserveth his soul.

18 Pride goeth before destruction, and an haughty spirit before a fall.

19 Better it is to be of an humble spirit with the lowly, than to divide the spoil with the proud.

20 He that handleth a matter wisely shall find good: and whoso trusteth in the Lord, happy is he.

21 The wise in heart shall be called prudent: and the sweetness of the lips increaseth learning.

22 Understanding is a wellspring of life unto him that hath it: but the instruction of fools is folly.

23 The heart of the wise teacheth his mouth, and addeth learning to his lips.

24 Pleasant words are as an honeycomb, sweet to the

laborat sibi quia conpulit eum os suum

27. vir impius fodit malum et in labiis eius ignis ardescit

28. homo perversus suscitat lites et verbosus separat principes

29. vir iniquus lactat amicum suum et ducit eum per viam non bonam

30. qui adtonitis oculis cogitat prava mordens labia sua perficit malum

31. corona dignitatis senectus in viis iustitiae repperietur

32. melior est patiens viro forte et qui dominatur animo suo expugnatore urbium

33. sortes mittuntur in sinu sed a Domino temperantur

soul, and health to the bones.

25 There is a way that seemeth right unto a man, but the end thereof are the ways of death.

26 He that laboureth laboureth for himself; for his mouth craveth it of him.

27 An ungodly man diggeth up evil: and in his lips there is as a burning fire.

28 A froward man soweth strife: and a whisperer separateth chief friends.

29 A violent man enticeth his neighbour, and leadeth him into the way that is not good.

30 He shutteth his eyes to devise froward things: moving his lips he bringeth evil to pass.

31 The hoary head is a crown of glory, if it be found in the way of righteousness.

32 He that is slow to anger is better than the mighty; and he that ruleth his spirit than he that taketh a city.

33 The lot is cast into the lap; but the whole disposing thereof is of the Lord.

CHAPTER 17

CHAPTER 17

1. melior est buccella sicca cum gaudio quam domus plena victimis cum iurgio

2. servus sapiens dominabitur filiis stultis et inter fratres hereditatem dividet

3. sicut igne probatur argentum et aurum camino ita corda probat Dominus

4. malus oboedit linguae iniquae et fallax obtemperat labiis mendacibus

5. qui despicit pauperem exprobrat factori eius et qui in ruina laetatur alterius non erit inpunitus

6. corona senum filii filiorum et gloria filiorum patres sui

7. non decent stultum verba conposita nec principem labium mentiens

8. gemma gratissima expectatio praestolantis quocumque se verterit prudenter intellegit

9. qui celat delictum

BETTER is a dry morsel, and quietness therewith, than an house full of sacrifices with strife.

2 A wise servant shall have rule over a son that causeth shame, and shall have part of the inheritance among the brethren.

3 The fining pot is for silver, and the furnace for gold: but the Lord trieth the hearts.

4 A wicked doer giveth heed to false lips; and a liar giveth ear to a naughty tongue.

5 Whoso mocketh the poor reproacheth his Maker: and he that is glad at calamities shall not be unpunished.

6 Children's children are the crown of old men; and the glory of children are their fathers.

7 Excellent speech becometh not a fool: much less do lying lips a prince.

8 A gift is as a precious stone in the eyes of him that hath it: whithersoever it turneth, it prospereth.

9 He that covereth a transgression seeketh love;

quaerit amicitias qui altero sermone repetit separat foederatos

10. plus proficit correptio apud prudentem quam centum plagae apud stultum

11. semper iurgia quaerit malus angelus autem crudelis mittetur contra eum

12. expedit magis ursae occurrere raptis fetibus quam fatuo confidenti sibi in stultitia sua

13. qui reddit mala pro bonis non recedet malum de domo eius

14. qui dimittit aquam caput est iurgiorum et antequam patiatur contumeliam iudicium deserit

15. et qui iustificat impium et qui condemnat iustum abominabilis est uterque apud Dominum

16. quid prodest habere divitias stultum cum sapientiam emere non possit

17. omni tempore diligit qui amicus est et frater in angustiis conprobatur

18. homo stultus plaudet manibus cum spoponderit

but he that repeateth a matter separateth very friends.

10 A reproof entereth more into a wise man than an hundred stripes into a fool.

11 An evil man seeketh only rebellion: therefore a cruel messenger shall be sent against him.

12 Let a bear robbed of her whelps meet a man, rather than a fool in his folly.

13 Whoso rewardeth evil for good, evil shall not depart from his house.

14 The beginning of strife is as when one letteth out water: therefore leave off contention, before it be meddled with.

15 He that justifieth the wicked, and he that condemneth the just, even they both are abomination to the Lord.

16 Wherefore is there a price in the hand of a fool to get wisdom, seeing he hath no heart to it?

17 A friend loveth at all times, and a brother is born for adversity.

18 A man void of understanding striketh hands, and becometh surety in the presence of his friend.

pro amico suo

19. qui meditatur discordiam diligit rixas et qui exaltat ostium quaerit ruinam

20. qui perversi cordis est non inveniet bonum et qui vertit linguam incidet in malum

21. natus est stultus in ignominiam suam sed nec pater in fatuo laetabitur

22. animus gaudens aetatem floridam facit spiritus tristis exsiccat ossa

23. munera de sinu impius accipit ut pervertat semitas iudicii

24. in facie prudentis lucet sapientia oculi stultorum in finibus terrae

25. ira patris filius stultus et dolor matris quae genuit eum

26. non est bonum damnum inferre iusto nec percutere principem qui recta iudicat

27. qui moderatur sermones suos doctus et prudens est et pretiosi spiritus vir eruditus

28. stultus quoque si tacuerit sapiens putabitur et si conpresserit labia

19 He loveth transgression that loveth strife: and he that exalteth his gate seeketh destruction.

20 He that hath a froward heart findeth no good: and he that hath a perverse tongue falleth into mischief.

21 He that begetteth a fool doeth it to his sorrow: and the father of a fool hath no joy.

22 A merry heart doeth good like a medicine: but a broken spirit drieth the bones.

23 A wicked man taketh a gift out of the bosom to pervert the ways of judgment.

24 Wisdom is before him that hath understanding; but the eyes of a fool are in the ends of the earth.

25 A foolish son is a grief to his father, and bitterness to her that bare him.

26 Also to punish the just is not good, nor to strike princes for equity.

27 He that hath knowledge spareth his words: and a man of understanding is of an excellent spirit.

28 Even a fool, when he holdeth his peace, is counted wise: and he that shutteth his

sua intellegens

lips is esteemed a man of understanding.

CHAPTER 18

1. occasiones quaerit qui vult recedere ab amico omni tempore erit exprobrabilis
2. non recipit stultus verba prudentiae nisi ea dixeris quae versantur in corde eius
3. impius cum in profundum venerit peccatorum contemnit sed sequitur eum ignominia et obprobrium
4. aqua profunda verba ex ore viri et torrens redundans fons sapientiae
5. accipere personam impii non est bonum ut declines a veritate iudicii
6. labia stulti inmiscunt se rixis et os eius iurgia provocat
7. os stulti contritio eius et labia illius ruina animae eius
8. verba bilinguis quasi simplicia et ipsa perveniunt usque ad interiora ventris
9. qui mollis et dissolutus est in opere suo frater est

CHAPTER 18

THROUGH desire a man, having separated himself, seeketh and intermeddleth with all wisdom.

2 A fool hath no delight in understanding, but that his heart may discover itself.

3 When the wicked cometh, then cometh also contempt, and with ignominy reproach.

4 The words of a man's mouth are as deep waters, and the wellspring of wisdom as a flowing brook.

5 It is not good to accept the person of the wicked, to overthrow the righteous in judgment.

6 A fool's lips enter into contention, and his mouth calleth for strokes.

7 A fool's mouth is his destruction, and his lips are the snare of his soul.

8 The words of a talebearer are as wounds, and they go down into the innermost parts of the belly.

9 He also that is slothful in his work is brother to him that is a great waster.

sua opera dissipantis

10. turris fortissima nomen Domini ad ipsum currit iustus et exaltabitur

11. substantia divitis urbs roboris eius et quasi murus validus circumdans eum

12. antequam conteratur exaltatur cor hominis et antequam glorificetur humiliatur

13. qui prius respondit quam audiat stultum se esse demonstrat et confusione dignum

14. spiritus viri sustentat inbecillitatem suam spiritum vero ad irascendum facilem quis poterit sustinere

15. cor prudens possidebit scientiam et auris sapientium quaerit doctrinam

16. donum hominis dilatat viam eius et ante principes spatium ei facit

17. iustus prior est accusator sui venit amicus eius et investigavit eum

18. contradictiones conprimit sors et inter potentes quoque diiudicat

19. frater qui adiuvatur a

10 The name of the Lord is a strong tower: the righteous runneth into it, and is safe.

11 The rich man's wealth is his strong city, and as an high wall in his own conceit.

12 Before destruction the heart of man is haughty, and before honour is humility.

13 He that answereth a matter before he heareth it, it is folly and shame unto him.

14 The spirit of a man will sustain his infirmity; but a wounded spirit who can bear?

15 The heart of the prudent getteth knowledge; and the ear of the wise seeketh knowledge.

16 A man's gift maketh room for him, and bringeth him before great men.

17 He that is first in his own cause seemeth just; but his neighbour cometh and searcheth him.

18 The lot causeth contentions to cease, and parteth between the mighty.

19 A brother offended is harder to be won than a strong city: and their contentions are like the bars of a castle.

20 A man's belly shall be

fratre quasi civitas firma et iudicia quasi vectes urbium

20. de fructu oris viri replebitur venter eius et genimina labiorum illius saturabunt eum

21. mors et vita in manu linguae qui diligunt eam comedent fructus eius

22. qui invenit mulierem invenit bonum et hauriet iucunditatem a Domino

23. cum obsecrationibus loquetur pauper et dives effabitur rigide

24. vir amicalis ad societatem magis amicus erit quam frater

satisfied with the fruit of his mouth; and with the increase of his lips shall he be filled.

21 Death and life are in the power of the tongue: and they that love it shall eat the fruit thereof.

22 Whoso findeth a wife findeth a good thing, and obtaineth favour of the Lord.

23 The poor useth intreaties; but the rich answereth roughly.

24 A man that hath friends must shew himself friendly: and there is a friend that sticketh closer than a brother.

CHAPTER 19

CHAPTER 19

1. melior est pauper qui ambulat in simplicitate sua quam torquens labia insipiens

2. ubi non est scientia animae non est bonum et qui festinus est pedibus offendit

3. stultitia hominis subplantat gressus eius et contra Deum fervet animo suo

4. divitiae addunt amicos

BETTER is the poor that walketh in his integrity, than he that is perverse in his lips, and is a fool.

2 Also, that the soul be without knowledge, it is not good; and he that hasteth with his feet sinneth.

3 The foolishness of man perverteth his way: and his heart fretteth against the Lord.

4 Wealth maketh many

plurimos a paupere autem et hii quos habuit separantur

5. testis falsus non erit inpunitus et qui mendacia loquitur non effugiet

6. multi colunt personam potentis et amici sunt dona tribuenti

7. fratres hominis pauperis oderunt eum insuper et amici procul recesserunt ab eo qui tantum verba sectatur nihil habebit

8. qui autem possessor est mentis diligit animam suam et custos prudentiae inveniet bona

9. testis falsus non erit inpunitus et qui loquitur mendacia peribit

10. non decent stultum deliciae nec servum dominari principibus

11. doctrina viri per patientiam noscitur et gloria eius est iniqua praetergredi

12. sicut fremitus leonis ita et regis ira et sicut ros super herbam ita hilaritas eius

13. dolor patris filius stultus et tecta iugiter perstillantia litigiosa

friends; but the poor is separated from his neighbour.

5 A false witness shall not be unpunished, and he that speaketh lies shall not escape.

6 Many will intreat the favour of the prince: and every man is a friend to him that giveth gifts.

7 All the brethren of the poor do hate him: how much more do his friends go far from him? he pursueth them with words, yet they are wanting to him.

8 He that getteth wisdom loveth his own soul: he that keepeth understanding shall find good.

9 A false witness shall not be unpunished, and he that speaketh lies shall perish.

10 Delight is not seemly for a fool; much less for a servant to have rule over princes.

11 The discretion of a man deferreth his anger; and it is his glory to pass over a transgression.

12 The king's wrath is as the roaring of a lion; but his favour is as dew upon the grass.

13 A foolish son is the

mulier

14. domus et divitiae dantur a patribus a Domino autem proprie uxor prudens

15. pigredo inmittit soporem et anima dissoluta esuriet

16. qui custodit mandatum custodit animam suam qui autem neglegit vias suas mortificabitur

17. feneratur Domino qui miseretur pauperis et vicissitudinem suam reddet ei

18. erudi filium tuum ne desperes ad interfectionem autem eius ne ponas animam tuam

19. qui inpatiens est sustinebit damnum et cum rapuerit aliud adponet

20. audi consilium et suscipe disciplinam ut sis sapiens in novissimis tuis

21. multae cogitationes in corde viri voluntas autem Domini permanebit

22. homo indigens misericors est et melior pauper quam vir mendax

23. timor Domini ad vitam et in plenitudine

calamity of his father: and the contentions of a wife are a continual dropping.

14 House and riches are the inheritance of fathers: and a prudent wife is from the Lord.

15 Slothfulness casteth into a deep sleep; and an idle soul shall suffer hunger.

16 He that keepeth the commandment keepeth his own soul; but he that despiseth his ways shall die.

17 He that hath pity upon the poor lendeth unto the Lord; and that which he hath given will he pay him again.

18 Chasten thy son while there is hope, and let not thy soul spare for his crying.

19 A man of great wrath shall suffer punishment: for if thou deliver him, yet thou must do it again.

20 Hear counsel, and receive instruction, that thou mayest be wise in thy latter end.

21 There are many devices in a man's heart; nevertheless the counsel of the Lord, that shall stand.

22 The desire of a man is his kindness: and a poor man is better than a liar.

23 The fear of the Lord

commorabitur absque visitatione pessimi

24. abscondit piger manum suam sub ascella nec ad os suum adplicat eam

25. pestilente flagellato stultus sapientior erit sin autem corripueris sapientem intelleget disciplinam

26. qui adfligit patrem et fugat matrem ignominiosus est et infelix

27. non cesses fili audire doctrinam nec ignores sermones scientiae

28. testis iniquus deridet iudicium et os impiorum devorat iniquitatem

29. parata sunt derisoribus iudicia et mallei percutientes stultorum corporibus

tendeth to life: and he that hath it shall abide satisfied; he shall not be visited with evil.

24 A slothful man hideth his hand in his bosom, and will not so much as bring it to his mouth again.

25 Smite a scorner, and the simple will beware: and reprove one that hath understanding, and he will understand knowledge.

26 He that wasteth his father, and chaseth away his mother, is a son that causeth shame, and bringeth reproach.

27 Cease, my son, to hear the instruction that causeth to err from the words of knowledge.

28 An ungodly witness scorneth judgment: and the mouth of the wicked devoureth iniquity.

29 Judgments are prepared for scorners, and stripes for the back of fools.

CHAPTER 20

CHAPTER 20

1. luxuriosa res vinum et tumultuosa ebrietas quicumque his delectatur non erit sapiens

WINE is a mocker, strong drink is raging: and whosoever is deceived thereby is not wise.

2. sicut rugitus leonis ita terror regis qui provocat eum peccat in animam suam

3. honor est homini qui separat se a contentionibus omnes autem stulti miscentur contumeliis

4. propter frigus piger arare noluit mendicabit ergo aestate et non dabitur ei

5. sicut aqua profunda sic consilium in corde viri sed homo sapiens exhauriet illud

6. multi homines misericordes vocantur virum autem fidelem quis inveniet

7. iustus qui ambulat in simplicitate sua beatos post se filios derelinquet

8. rex qui sedet in solio iudicii dissipat omne malum intuitu suo

9. quis potest dicere mundum est cor meum purus sum a peccato

10. pondus et pondus mensura et mensura utrumque abominabile est apud Deum

11. ex studiis suis intellegitur puer si munda

2 The fear of a king is as the roaring of a lion: whoso provoketh him to anger sinneth against his own soul.

3 It is an honour for a man to cease from strife: but every fool will be meddling.

4 The sluggard will not plow by reason of the cold; therefore shall he beg in harvest, and have nothing.

5 Counsel in the heart of man is like deep water; but a man of understanding will draw it out.

6 Most men will proclaim every one his own goodness: but a faithful man who can find?

7 The just man walketh in his integrity: his children are blessed after him.

8 A king that sitteth in the throne of judgment scattereth away all evil with his eyes.

9 Who can say, I have made my heart clean, I am pure from my sin?

10 Divers weights, and divers measures, both of them are alike abomination to the Lord.

11 Even a child is known by his doings, whether his work be pure, and whether it be right.

et si recta sint opera eius

12. aurem audientem et oculum videntem Dominus fecit utrumque

13. noli diligere somnum ne te egestas opprimat aperi oculos tuos et saturare panibus

14. malum est malum est dicit omnis emptor et cum recesserit tunc gloriabitur

15. est aurum et multitudo gemmarum vas autem pretiosum labia scientiae

16. tolle vestimentum eius qui fideiussor extitit alieni et pro extraneis aufer pignus ab eo

17. suavis est homini panis mendacii et postea implebitur os eius calculo

18. cogitationes consiliis roborantur et gubernaculis tractanda sunt bella

19. ei qui revelat mysteria et ambulat fraudulenter et dilatat labia sua ne commiscearis

20. qui maledicit patri suo et matri extinguetur lucerna eius in mediis tenebris

21. hereditas ad quam

12 The hearing ear, and the seeing eye, the Lord hath made even both of them.

13 Love not sleep, lest thou come to poverty; open thine eyes, and thou shalt be satisfied with bread.

14 It is naught, it is naught, saith the buyer: but when he is gone his way, then he boasteth.

15 There is gold, and a multitude of rubies: but the lips of knowledge are a precious jewel.

16 Take his garment that is surety for a stranger: and take a pledge of him for a strange woman.

17 Bread of deceit is sweet to a man; but afterwards his mouth shall be filled with gravel.

18 Every purpose is established by counsel: and with good advice make war.

19 He that goeth about as a talebearer revealeth secrets: therefore meddle not with him that flattereth with his lips.

20 Whoso curseth his father or his mother, his lamp shall be put out in obscure darkness.

21 An inheritance may be

festinatur in principio in novissimo benedictione carebit

22. ne dicas reddam malum expecta Dominum et liberabit te

23. abominatio est apud Deum pondus et pondus statera dolosa non est bona

24. a Domino diriguntur gressus viri quis autem hominum intellegere potest viam suam

25. ruina est hominis devorare sanctos et post vota tractare

26. dissipat impios rex sapiens et curvat super eos fornicem

27. lucerna Domini spiraculum hominis quae investigat omnia secreta ventris

28. misericordia et veritas custodiunt regem et roboratur clementia thronus eius

29. exultatio iuvenum fortitudo eorum et dignitas senum canities

30. livor vulneris absterget mala et plagae in secretioribus ventris

gotten hastily at the beginning; but the end thereof shall not be blessed.

22 Say not thou, I will recompense evil; but wait on the Lord, and he shall save thee.

23 Divers weights are an abomination unto the Lord; and a false balance is not good.

24 Man's goings are of the Lord; how can a man then understand his own way?

25 It is a snare to the man who devoureth that which is holy, and after vows to make inquiry.

26 A wise king scattereth the wicked, and bringeth the wheel over them.

27 The spirit of man is the candle of the Lord, searching all the inward parts of the belly.

28 Mercy and truth preserve the king: and his throne is upholden by mercy.

29 The glory of young men is their strength: and the beauty of old men is the gray head.

30 The blueness of a wound cleanseth away evil: so do stripes the inward parts of the belly.

1. sicut divisiones aquarum ita cor regis in manu Domini quocumque voluerit inclinabit illud

2. omnis via viri recta sibi videtur adpendit autem corda Dominus

3. facere misericordiam et iudicium magis placent Domino quam victimae

4. exaltatio oculorum et dilatatio cordis lucerna impiorum peccatum

5. cogitationes robusti semper in abundantia omnis autem piger semper in egestate

6. qui congregat thesauros lingua mendacii vanus est et inpingetur ad laqueos mortis

7. rapinae impiorum detrahent eos quia noluerunt facere iudicium

8. perversa via viri aliena est qui autem mundus est rectum opus eius

9. melius est sedere in angulo domatis quam cum muliere litigiosa et in domo communi

10. anima impii desiderat malum non miserebitur

THE king's heart is in the hand of the Lord, as the rivers of water: he turneth it whithersoever he will.

2 Every way of a man is right in his own eyes: but the Lord pondereth the hearts.

3 To do justice and judgment is more acceptable to the Lord than sacrifice.

4 An high look, and a proud heart, and the plowing of the wicked, is sin.

5 The thoughts of the diligent tend only to plenteousness; but of every one that is hasty only to want.

6 The getting of treasures by a lying tongue is a vanity tossed to and fro of them that seek death.

7 The robbery of the wicked shall destroy them; because they refuse to do judgment.

8 The way of man is froward and strange: but as for the pure, his work is right.

9 It is better to dwell in a corner of the housetop, than with a brawling woman in a wide house.

10 The soul of the wicked desireth evil: his neighbour

proximo suo

11. multato pestilente sapientior erit parvulus et si sectetur sapientem sumet scientiam

12. excogitat iustus de domo impii ut detrahat impios in malum

13. qui obturat aurem suam ad clamorem pauperis et ipse clamabit et non exaudietur

14. munus absconditum extinguet iras et donum in sinu indignationem maximam

15. gaudium iusto est facere iudicium et pavor operantibus iniquitatem

16. vir qui erraverit a via doctrinae in coetu gigantum commorabitur

17. qui diligit epulas in egestate erit qui amat vinum et pinguia non ditabitur

18. pro iusto datur impius et pro rectis iniquus

19. melius est habitare in terra deserta quam cum muliere rixosa et iracunda

20. thesaurus desiderabilis et oleum in habitaculo iusti et inprudens homo dissipabit illud

findeth no favour in his eyes.

11 When the scorner is punished, the simple is made wise: and when the wise is instructed, he receiveth knowledge.

12 The righteous man wisely considereth the house of the wicked: but God overthroweth the wicked for their wickedness.

13 Whoso stoppeth his ears at the cry of the poor, he also shall cry himself, but shall not be heard.

14 A gift in secret pacifieth anger: and a reward in the bosom strong wrath.

15 It is joy to the just to do judgment: but destruction shall be to the workers of iniquity.

16 The man that wandereth out of the way of understanding shall remain in the congregation of the dead.

17 He that loveth pleasure shall be a poor man: he that loveth wine and oil shall not be rich.

18 The wicked shall be a ransom for the righteous, and the transgressor for the upright.

19 It is better to dwell in the wilderness, than with a

21. qui sequitur iustitiam et misericordiam inveniet vitam et iustitiam et gloriam

22. civitatem fortium ascendit sapiens et destruxit robur fiduciae eius

23. qui custodit os suum et linguam suam custodit ab angustiis animam suam

24. superbus et arrogans vocatur indoctus qui in ira operatur superbiam

25. desideria occidunt pigrum noluerunt enim quicquam manus eius operari

26. tota die concupiscit et desiderat qui autem iustus est tribuet et non cessabit

27. hostiae impiorum abominabiles quia offeruntur ex scelere

28. testis mendax peribit vir oboediens loquitur victoriam

29. vir impius procaciter obfirmat vultum suum qui autem rectus est corrigit viam suam

30. non est sapientia non est prudentia non est consilium contra Dominum

contentious and an angry woman.

20 There is treasure to be desired and oil in the dwelling of the wise; but a foolish man spendeth it up.

21 He that followeth after righteousness and mercy findeth life, righteousness, and honour.

22 A wise man scaleth the city of the mighty, and casteth down the strength of the confidence thereof.

23 Whoso keepeth his mouth and his tongue keepeth his soul from troubles.

24 Proud and haughty scorner is his name, who dealeth in proud wrath.

25 The desire of the slothful killeth him; for his hands refuse to labour.

26 He coveteth greedily all the day long: but the righteous giveth and spareth not.

27 The sacrifice of the wicked is abomination: how much more, when he bringeth it with a wicked mind?

28 A false witness shall perish: but the man that heareth speaketh constantly.

29 A wicked man hardeneth

31. equus paratur ad diem belli Dominus autem salutem tribuet

his face: but as for the upright, he directeth his way.

30 There is no wisdom nor understanding nor counsel against the Lord.

31 The horse is prepared against the day of battle: but safety is of the Lord.

CHAPTER 22

CHAPTER 22

1. melius est nomen bonum quam divitiae multae super argentum et aurum gratia bona
2. dives et pauper obviaverunt sibi utriusque operator est Dominus
3. callidus vidit malum et abscondit se innocens pertransiit et adflictus est damno
4. finis modestiae timor Domini divitiae et gloria et vita
5. arma et gladii in via perversi custos animae suae longe recedit ab eis
6. proverbium est adulescens iuxta viam suam etiam cum senuerit non recedet ab ea
7. dives pauperibus imperat et qui accipit

A GOOD name is rather to be chosen than great riches, and loving favour rather than silver and gold.

2 The rich and poor meet together: the Lord is the maker of them all.

3 A prudent man foreseeth the evil, and hideth himself: but the simple pass on, and are punished.

4 By humility and the fear of the Lord are riches, and honour, and life.

5 Thorns and snares are in the way of the froward: he that doth keep his soul shall be far from them.

6 Train up a child in the way he should go: and when he is old, he will not depart from it.

7 The rich ruleth over the poor, and the borrower is

mutuum servus est fenerantis

8. qui seminat iniquitatem metet mala et virga irae suae consummabitur

9. qui pronus est ad misericordiam benedicetur de panibus enim suis dedit pauperi

10. eice derisorem et exibit cum eo iurgium cessabuntque causae et contumeliae

11. qui diligit cordis munditiam propter gratiam labiorum suorum habebit amicum regem

12. oculi Domini custodiunt scientiam et subplantantur verba iniqui

13. dicit piger leo foris in medio platearum occidendus sum

14. fovea profunda os alienae cui iratus est Dominus incidet in eam

15. stultitia conligata est in corde pueri et virga disciplinae fugabit eam

16. qui calumniatur pauperem ut augeat divitias suas dabit ipse ditiori et egebit

17. inclina aurem tuam et audi verba sapientium

servant to the lender.

8 He that soweth iniquity shall reap vanity: and the rod of his anger shall fail.

9 He that hath a bountiful eye shall be blessed; for he giveth of his bread to the poor.

10 Cast out the scorner, and contention shall go out; yea, strife and reproach shall cease.

11 He that loveth pureness of heart, for the grace of his lips the king shall be his friend.

12 The eyes of the Lord preserve knowledge, and he overthroweth the words of the transgressor.

13 The slothful man saith, There is a lion without, I shall be slain in the streets.

14 The mouth of strange women is a deep pit: he that is abhorred of the Lord shall fall therein.

15 Foolishness is bound in the heart of a child; but the rod of correction shall drive it far from him.

16 He that oppresseth the poor to increase his riches, and he that giveth to the rich, shall surely come to want.

17 Bow down thine ear, and hear the words of the wise,

adpone autem cor ad doctrinam meam

18. quae pulchra erit tibi cum servaveris eam in ventre tuo et redundabit in labiis tuis

19. ut sit in Domino fiducia tua unde et ostendi eam tibi hodie

20. ecce descripsi eam tibi tripliciter in cogitationibus et scientia

21. ut ostenderem tibi firmitatem et eloquia veritatis respondere ex his illi qui misit te

22. non facias violentiam pauperi quia pauper est neque conteras egenum in porta

23. quia Dominus iudicabit causam eius et configet eos qui confixerint animam eius

24. noli esse amicus homini iracundo neque ambules cum viro furioso

25. ne forte discas semitas eius et sumas scandalum animae tuae

26. noli esse cum his qui defigunt manus suas et qui vades se offerunt pro debitis

27. si enim non habes unde restituas quid

and apply thine heart unto my knowledge.

18 For it is a pleasant thing if thou keep them within thee; they shall withal be fitted in thy lips.

19 That thy trust may be in the Lord, I have made known to thee this day, even to thee.

20 Have not I written to thee excellent things in counsels and knowledge,

21 That I might make thee know the certainty of the words of truth; that thou mightest answer the words of truth to them that send unto thee?

22 Rob not the poor, because he is poor: neither oppress the afflicted in the gate:

23 For the Lord will plead their cause, and spoil the soul of those that spoiled them.

24 Make no friendship with an angry man; and with a furious man thou shalt not go:

25 Lest thou learn his ways, and get a snare to thy soul.

26 Be not thou one of them that strike hands, or of them that are sureties for debts.

27 If thou hast nothing to pay, why should he take away thy bed from under

causae est ut tollat operimentum de cubili tuo

28. ne transgrediaris terminos antiquos quos posuerunt patres tui

29. vidisti virum velocem in opere suo coram regibus stabit nec erit ante ignobiles

thee?

28 Remove not the ancient landmark, which thy fathers have set.

29 Seest thou a man diligent in his business? he shall stand before kings; he shall not stand before mean men.

CHAPTER 23

1. quando sederis ut comedas cum principe diligenter adtende quae posita sunt ante faciem tuam

2. et statue cultrum in gutture tuo si tamen habes in potestate animam tuam

3. ne desideres de cibis eius in quo est panis mendacii

4. noli laborare ut diteris sed prudentiae tuae pone modum

5. ne erigas oculos tuos ad opes quas habere non potes quia facient sibi pinnas quasi aquilae et avolabunt in caelum

6. ne comedas cum homine invido et ne

CHAPTER 23

WHEN thou sittest to eat with a ruler, consider diligently what is before thee:

2 And put a knife to thy throat, if thou be a man given to appetite.

3 Be not desirous of his dainties: for they are deceitful meat.

4 Labour not to be rich: cease from thine own wisdom.

5 Wilt thou set thine eyes upon that which is not? for riches certainly make themselves wings; they fly away as an eagle toward heaven.

6 Eat thou not the bread of him that hath an evil eye, neither desire thou his dainty meats:

desideres cibos eius

7. quoniam in similitudinem arioli et coniectoris aestimat quod ignorat comede et bibe dicet tibi et mens eius non est tecum

8. cibos quos comederas evomes et perdes pulchros sermones tuos

9. in auribus insipientium ne loquaris quia despicient doctrinam eloquii tui

10. ne adtingas terminos parvulorum et agrum pupillorum ne introeas

11. propinquus enim eorum Fortis est et ipse iudicabit contra te causam illorum

12. ingrediatur ad doctrinam cor tuum et aures tuae ad verba scientiae

13. noli subtrahere a puero disciplinam si enim percusseris eum virga non morietur

14. tu virga percuties eum et animam eius de inferno liberabis

15. fili mi si sapiens fuerit animus tuus gaudebit tecum cor meum

16. et exultabunt renes

7 For as he thinketh in his heart, so is he: Eat and drink, saith he to thee; but his heart is not with thee.

8 The morsel which thou hast eaten shalt thou vomit up, and lose thy sweet words.

9 Speak not in the ears of a fool: for he will despise the wisdom of thy words.

10 Remove not the old landmark; and enter not into the fields of the fatherless:

11 For their redeemer is mighty; he shall plead their cause with thee.

12 Apply thine heart unto instruction, and thine ears to the words of knowledge.

13 Withhold not correction from the child: for if thou beatest him with the rod, he shall not die.

14 Thou shalt beat him with the rod, and shalt deliver his soul from hell.

15 My son, if thine heart be wise, my heart shall rejoice, even mine.

16 Yea, my reins shall rejoice, when thy lips speak right things.

17 Let not thine heart envy sinners: but be thou in the fear of the Lord all the day long.

mei cum locuta fuerint rectum labia tua

17. non aemuletur cor tuum peccatores sed in timore Domini esto tota die

18. quia habebis spem in novissimo et praestolatio tua non auferetur

19. audi fili mi et esto sapiens et dirige in via animum tuum

20. noli esse in conviviis potatorum nec in comesationibus eorum qui carnes ad vescendum conferunt

21. quia vacantes potibus et dantes symbola consumentur et vestietur pannis dormitatio

22. audi patrem tuum qui genuit te et ne contemnas cum senuerit mater tua

23. veritatem eme et noli vendere sapientiam et doctrinam et intellegentiam

24. exultat gaudio pater iusti qui sapientem genuit laetabitur in eo

25. gaudeat pater tuus et mater tua et exultet quae genuit te

26. praebe fili mi cor tuum mihi et oculi tui

18 For surely there is an end; and thine expectation shall not be cut off.

19 Hear thou, my son, and be wise, and guide thine heart in the way.

20 Be not among winebibbers; among riotous eaters of flesh:

21 For the drunkard and the glutton shall come to poverty: and drowsiness shall clothe a man with rags.

22 Hearken unto thy father that begat thee, and despise not thy mother when she is old.

23 Buy the truth, and sell it not; also wisdom, and instruction, and understanding.

24 The father of the righteous shall greatly rejoice: and he that begetteth a wise child shall have joy of him.

25 Thy father and thy mother shall be glad, and she that bare thee shall rejoice.

26 My son, give me thine heart, and let thine eyes observe my ways.

27 For a whore is a deep ditch; and a strange woman is a narrow pit.

28 She also lieth in wait as

vias meas custodiant

27. fovea enim profunda est meretrix et puteus angustus aliena

28. insidiatur in via quasi latro et quos incautos viderit interficit

29. cui vae cuius patri vae cui rixae cui foveae cui sine causa vulnera cui suffusio oculorum

30. nonne his qui morantur in vino et student calicibus epotandis

31. ne intuearis vinum quando flavescit cum splenduerit in vitro color eius ingreditur blande

32. sed in novissimo mordebit ut coluber et sicut regulus venena diffundet

33. oculi tui videbunt extraneas et cor tuum loquetur perversa

34. et eris sicut dormiens in medio mari et quasi sopitus gubernator amisso clavo

35. et dices verberaverunt me sed non dolui traxerunt me et ego non sensi quando evigilabo et rursum vina repperiam

for a prey, and increaseth the transgressors among men.

29 Who hath woe? who hath sorrow? who hath contentions? who hath babbling? who hath wounds without cause? who hath redness of eyes?

30 They that tarry long at the wine; they that go to seek mixed wine.

31 Look not thou upon the wine when it is red, when it giveth his colour in the cup, when it moveth itself aright.

32 At the last it biteth like a serpent, and stingeth like an adder.

33 Thine eyes shall behold strange women, and thine heart shall utter perverse things.

34 Yea, thou shalt be as he that lieth down in the midst of the sea, or as he that lieth upon the top of a mast.

35 They have stricken me, shalt thou say, and I was not sick; they have beaten me, and I felt it not: when shall I awake? I will seek it yet again.

1. ne aemuleris viros malos nec desideres esse cum eis

2. quia rapinas meditatur mens eorum et fraudes labia eorum loquuntur

3. sapientia aedificabitur domus et prudentia roborabitur

4. in doctrina replebuntur cellaria universa substantia pretiosa et pulcherrima

5. vir sapiens et fortis est et vir doctus robustus et validus

6. quia cum dispositione initur bellum et erit salus ubi multa consilia sunt

7. excelsa stulto sapientia in porta non aperiet os suum

8. qui cogitat malefacere stultus vocabitur

9. cogitatio stulti peccatum est et abominatio hominum detractor

10. si desperaveris lassus in die angustiae inminuetur fortitudo tua

11. erue eos qui ducuntur ad mortem et qui

BE not thou envious against evil men, neither desire to be with them.

2 For their heart studieth destruction, and their lips talk of mischief.

3 Through wisdom is an house builded; and by understanding it is established:

4 And by knowledge shall the chambers be filled with all precious and pleasant riches.

5 A wise man is strong; yea, a man of knowledge increaseth strength.

6 For by wise counsel thou shalt make thy war: and in multitude of counsellers there is safety.

7 Wisdom is too high for a fool: he openeth not his mouth in the gate.

8 He that deviseth to do evil shall be called a mischievous person.

9 The thought of foolishness is sin: and the scorner is an abomination to men.

10 If thou faint in the day of adversity, thy strength is small.

trahuntur ad interitum liberare ne cesses

12. si dixeris vires non suppetunt qui inspector est cordis ipse intellegit et servatorem animae tuae nihil fallit reddetque homini iuxta opera sua

13. comede fili mi mel quia bonum est et favum dulcissimum gutturi tuo

14. sic et doctrina sapientiae animae tuae quam cum inveneris habebis in novissimis et spes tua non peribit

15. ne insidieris et quaeras impietatem in domo iusti neque vastes requiem eius

16. septies enim cadet iustus et resurget impii autem corruent in malum

17. cum ceciderit inimicus tuus ne gaudeas et in ruina eius ne exultet cor tuum

18. ne forte videat Dominus et displiceat ei et auferat ab eo iram suam

19. ne contendas cum pessimis nec aemuleris impios

20. quoniam non habent futurorum spem mali et

11 If thou forbear to deliver them that are drawn unto death, and those that are ready to be slain;

12 If thou sayest, Behold, we knew it not; doth not he that pondereth the heart consider it? and he that keepeth thy soul, doth not he know it? and shall not he render to every man according to his works?

13 My son, eat thou honey, because it is good; and the honeycomb, which is sweet to thy taste:

14 So shall the knowledge of wisdom be unto thy soul: when thou hast found it, then there shall be a reward, and thy expectation shall not be cut off.

15 Lay not wait, O wicked man, against the dwelling of the righteous; spoil not his resting place:

16 For a just man falleth seven times, and riseth up again: but the wicked shall fall into mischief.

17 Rejoice not when thine enemy falleth, and let not thine heart be glad when he stumbleth:

18 Lest the Lord see it, and it displease him, and he turn

lucerna impiorum extinguetur

21. time Dominum fili mi et regem et cum detractoribus non commiscearis

22. quoniam repente consurget perditio eorum et ruinam utriusque quis novit

23. haec quoque sapientibus cognoscere personam in iudicio non est bonum

24. qui dicit impio iustus es maledicent ei populi et detestabuntur eum tribus

25. qui arguunt laudabuntur et super ipsos veniet benedictio

26. labia deosculabitur qui recta verba respondet

27. praepara foris opus tuum et diligenter exerce agrum tuum ut postea aedifices domum tuam

28. ne sis testis frustra contra proximum tuum nec lactes quemquam labiis tuis

29. ne dicas quomodo fecit mihi sic faciam ei reddam unicuique secundum opus suum

30. per agrum hominis pigri transivi et per

away his wrath from him.

19 Fret not thyself because of evil men, neither be thou envious at the wicked;

20 For there shall be no reward to the evil man; the candle of the wicked shall be put out.

21 My son, fear thou the Lord and the king: and meddle not with them that are given to change:

22 For their calamity shall rise suddenly; and who knoweth the ruin of them both?

23 These things also belong to the wise. It is not good to have respect of persons in judgment.

24 He that saith unto the wicked, Thou art righteous; him shall the people curse, nations shall abhor him:

25 But to them that rebuke him shall be delight, and a good blessing shall come upon them.

26 Every man shall kiss his lips that giveth a right answer.

27 Prepare thy work without, and make it fit for thyself in the field; and afterwards build thine house.

28 Be not a witness against

vineam viri stulti

31. et ecce totum repleverant urticae operuerant superficiem eius spinae et maceria lapidum destructa erat

32. quod cum vidissem posui in corde meo et exemplo didici disciplinam

33. parum inquam dormies modicum dormitabis pauxillum manus conseres ut quiescas

34. et veniet quasi cursor egestas tua et mendicitas quasi vir armatus

thy neighbour without cause; and deceive not with thy lips.

29 Say not, I will do so to him as he hath done to me: I will render to the man according to his work.

30 I went by the field of the slothful, and by the vineyard of the man void of understanding;

31 And, lo, it was all grown over with thorns, and nettles had covered the face thereof, and the stone wall thereof was broken down.

32 Then I saw, and considered it well: I looked upon it, and received instruction.

33 Yet a little sleep, a little slumber, a little folding of the hands to sleep:

34 So shall thy poverty come as one that travelleth; and thy want as an armed man.

CHAPTER 25

CHAPTER 25

1. haec quoque parabolae Salomonis quas transtulerunt viri Ezechiae regis Iuda

2. gloria Dei celare verbum et gloria regum investigare sermonem

THESE are also proverbs of Solomon, which the men of Hezekiah king of Judah copied out.

2 It is the glory of God to conceal a thing: but the honour of kings is to search

3. caelum sursum et terra deorsum et cor regum inscrutabile

4. aufer robiginem de argento et egredietur vas purissimum

5. aufer impietatem de vultu regis et firmabitur iustitia thronus eius

6. ne gloriosus appareas coram rege et in loco magnorum ne steteris

7. melius est enim ut dicatur tibi ascende huc quam ut humilieris coram principe

8. quae viderunt oculi tui ne proferas in iurgio cito ne postea emendare non possis cum dehonestaveris amicum tuum

9. causam tuam tracta cum amico tuo et secretum extraneo non reveles

10. ne forte insultet tibi cum audierit et exprobrare non cesset

11. mala aurea in lectis argenteis qui loquitur verbum in tempore suo

12. inauris aurea et margaritum fulgens qui arguit sapientem et aurem oboedientem

out a matter.

3 The heaven for height, and the earth for depth, and the heart of kings is unsearchable.

4 Take away the dross from the silver, and there shall come forth a vessel for the finer.

5 Take away the wicked from before the king, and his throne shall be established in righteousness.

6 Put not forth thyself in the presence of the king, and stand not in the place of great men:

7 For better it is that it be said unto thee, Come up hither; than that thou shouldest be put lower in the presence of the prince whom thine eyes have seen.

8 Go not forth hastily to strive, lest thou know not what to do in the end thereof, when thy neighbour hath put thee to shame.

9 Debate thy cause with thy neighbour himself; and discover not a secret to another:

10 Lest he that heareth it put thee to shame, and thine infamy turn not away.

11 A word fitly spoken is

13. sicut frigus nivis in die messis ita legatus fidelis ei qui misit eum animam illius requiescere facit

14. nubes et ventus et pluviae non sequentes vir gloriosus et promissa non conplens

15. patientia lenietur princeps et lingua mollis confringet duritiam

16. mel invenisti comede quod sufficit tibi ne forte saturatus evomas illud

17. subtrahe pedem tuum de domo proximi tui nequando satiatus oderit te

18. iaculum et gladius et sagitta acuta homo qui loquitur contra proximum suum testimonium falsum

19. dens putridus et pes lapsus qui sperat super infideli in die angustiae

20. et amittit pallium in die frigoris acetum in nitro et qui cantat carmina cordi pessimo

21. si esurierit inimicus tuus ciba illum et si sitierit da ei aquam bibere

22. prunam enim congregabis super caput eius et Dominus reddet

like apples of gold in pictures of silver.

12 As an earring of gold, and an ornament of fine gold, so is a wise reprover upon an obedient ear.

13 As the cold of snow in the time of harvest, so is a faithful messenger to them that send him: for he refresheth the soul of his masters.

14 Whoso boasteth himself of a false gift is like clouds and wind without rain.

15 By long forbearing is a prince persuaded, and a soft tongue breaketh the bone.

16 Hast thou found honey? eat so much as is sufficient for thee, lest thou be filled therewith, and vomit it.

17 Withdraw thy foot from thy neighbour's house; lest he be weary of thee, and so hate thee.

18 A man that beareth false witness against his neighbour is a maul, and a sword, and a sharp arrow.

19 Confidence in an unfaithful man in time of trouble is like a broken tooth, and a foot out of joint.

20 As he that taketh away a garment in cold weather, and

tibi

23. ventus aquilo dissipat pluvias et facies tristis linguam detrahentem

24. melius est sedere in angulo domatis quam cum muliere litigiosa et in domo communi

25. aqua frigida animae sitienti et nuntius bonus de terra longinqua

26. fons turbatus pede et vena corrupta iustus cadens coram impio

27. sicut qui mel multum comedit non est ei bonum sic qui scrutator est maiestatis opprimitur gloria

28. sicut urbs patens et absque murorum ambitu ita vir qui non potest in loquendo cohibere spiritum suum

as vinegar upon nitre, so is he that singeth songs to an heavy heart.

21 If thine enemy be hungry, give him bread to eat; and if he be thirsty, give him water to drink:

22 For thou shalt heap coals of fire upon his head, and the Lord shall reward thee.

23 The north wind driveth away rain: so doth an angry countenance a backbiting tongue.

24 It is better to dwell in the corner of the housetop, than with a brawling woman and in a wide house.

25 As cold waters to a thirsty soul, so is good news from a far country.

26 A righteous man falling down before the wicked is as a troubled fountain, and a corrupt spring.

27 It is not good to eat much honey: so for men to search their own glory is not glory.

28 He that hath no rule over his own spirit is like a city that is broken down, and without walls.

1. quomodo nix aestate et pluvia in messe sic indecens est stulto gloria

2. sicut avis ad alia transvolans et passer quolibet vadens sic maledictum frustra prolatum in quempiam superveniet

3. flagellum equo et camus asino et virga dorso inprudentium

4. ne respondeas stulto iuxta stultitiam suam ne efficiaris ei similis

5. responde stulto iuxta stultitiam suam ne sibi sapiens esse videatur

6. claudus pedibus et iniquitatem bibens qui mittit verba per nuntium stultum

7. quomodo pulchras frustra habet claudus tibias sic indecens est in ore stultorum parabola

8. sicut qui mittit lapidem in acervum Mercurii ita qui tribuit insipienti honorem

9. quomodo si spina nascatur in manu

AS snow in summer, and as rain in harvest, so honour is not seemly for a fool.

2 As the bird by wandering, as the swallow by flying, so the curse causeless shall not come.

3 A whip for the horse, a bridle for the ass, and a rod for the fool's back.

4 Answer not a fool according to his folly, lest thou also be like unto him.

5 Answer a fool according to his folly, lest he be wise in his own conceit.

6 He that sendeth a message by the hand of a fool cutteth off the feet, and drinketh damage.

7 The legs of the lame are not equal: so is a parable in the mouth of fools.

8 As he that bindeth a stone in a sling, so is he that giveth honour to a fool.

9 As a thorn goeth up into the hand of a drunkard, so is a parable in the mouth of fools.

10 The great God that formed all things both

temulenti sic parabola in ore stultorum

10. iudicium determinat causas et qui inponit stulto silentium iras mitigat

11. sicut canis qui revertitur ad vomitum suum sic inprudens qui iterat stultitiam suam

12. vidisti hominem sapientem sibi videri magis illo spem habebit stultus

13. dicit piger leaena in via leo in itineribus

14. sicut ostium vertitur in cardine suo ita piger in lectulo suo

15. abscondit piger manus sub ascellas suas et laborat si ad os suum eas converterit

16. sapientior sibi piger videtur septem viris loquentibus sententias

17. sicut qui adprehendit auribus canem sic qui transit et inpatiens commiscetur rixae alterius

18. sicut noxius est qui mittit lanceas et sagittas et mortem

19. sic vir qui fraudulenter nocet amico

rewardeth the fool, and rewardeth transgressors.

11 As a dog returneth to his vomit, so a fool returneth to his folly.

12 Seest thou a man wise in his own conceit? there is more hope of a fool than of him.

13 The slothful man saith, There is a lion in the way; a lion is in the streets.

14 As the door turneth upon his hinges, so doth the slothful upon his bed.

15 The slothful hideth his hand in his bosom; it grieveth him to bring it again to his mouth.

16 The sluggard is wiser in his own conceit than seven men that can render a reason.

17 He that passeth by, and meddleth with strife belonging not to him, is like one that taketh a dog by the ears.

18 As a mad man who casteth firebrands, arrows, and death,

19 So is the man that deceiveth his neighbour, and saith, Am not I in sport?

20 Where no wood is, there the fire goeth out: so where there is no talebearer, the

suo et cum fuerit deprehensus dicit ludens feci

20. cum defecerint ligna extinguetur ignis et susurrone subtracto iurgia conquiescunt

21. sicut carbones ad prunam et ligna ad ignem sic homo iracundus suscitat rixas

22. verba susurronis quasi simplicia et ipsa perveniunt ad intima ventris

23. quomodo si argento sordido ornare velis vas fictile sic labia tumentia cum pessimo corde sociata

24. labiis suis intellegitur inimicus cum in corde tractaverit dolos

25. quando submiserit vocem suam ne credideris ei quoniam septem nequitiae sunt in corde illius

26. qui operit odium fraudulenter revelabitur malitia eius in concilio

27. qui fodit foveam incidet in eam et qui volvit lapidem revertetur ad eum

28. lingua fallax non

strife ceaseth.

21 As coals are to burning coals, and wood to fire; so is a contentious man to kindle strife.

22 The words of a talebearer are as wounds, and they go down into the innermost parts of the belly.

23 Burning lips and a wicked heart are like a potsherd covered with silver dross.

24 He that hateth dissembleth with his lips, and layeth up deceit within him;

25 When he speaketh fair, believe him not: for there are seven abominations in his heart.

26 Whose hatred is covered by deceit, his wickedness shall be shewed before the whole congregation.

27 Whoso diggeth a pit shall fall therein: and he that rolleth a stone, it will return upon him.

28 A lying tongue hateth those that are afflicted by it; and a flattering mouth worketh ruin.

amat veritatem et os lubricum operatur ruinas

CHAPTER 27

1. ne glorieris in crastinum ignorans quid superventura pariat dies
2. laudet te alienus et non os tuum extraneus et non labia tua
3. grave est saxum et onerosa harena sed ira stulti utroque gravior
4. ira non habet misericordiam nec erumpens furor et impetum concitati ferre quis poterit
5. melior est manifesta correptio quam amor absconditus
6. meliora sunt vulnera diligentis quam fraudulenta odientis oscula
7. anima saturata calcabit favum anima esuriens et amarum pro dulce sumet
8. sicut avis transmigrans de nido suo sic vir qui relinquit locum suum
9. unguento et variis odoribus delectatur cor et bonis amici consiliis

CHAPTER 27

BOAST not thyself of to morrow; for thou knowest not what a day may bring forth.

2 Let another man praise thee, and not thine own mouth; a stranger, and not thine own lips.

3 A stone is heavy, and the sand weighty; but a fool's wrath is heavier than them both.

4 Wrath is cruel, and anger is outrageous; but who is able to stand before envy?

5 Open rebuke is better than secret love.

6 Faithful are the wounds of a friend; but the kisses of an enemy are deceitful.

7 The full soul loatheth an honeycomb; but to the hungry soul every bitter thing is sweet.

8 As a bird that wandereth from her nest, so is a man that wandereth from his place.

9 Ointment and perfume rejoice the heart: so doth the

anima dulcoratur

10. amicum tuum et amicum patris tui ne dimiseris et domum fratris tui ne ingrediaris in die adflictionis tuae melior est vicinus iuxta quam frater procul

11. stude sapientiae fili mi et laetifica cor meum ut possim exprobranti respondere sermonem

12. astutus videns malum absconditus est parvuli transeuntes sustinuere dispendia

13. tolle vestimentum eius qui spopondit pro extraneo et pro alienis auferto pignus

14. qui benedicit proximo suo voce grandi de nocte consurgens maledicenti similis erit

15. tecta perstillantia in die frigoris et litigiosa mulier conparantur

16. qui retinet eam quasi qui ventum teneat et oleum dexterae suae vocabit

17. ferrum ferro acuitur et homo exacuit faciem amici sui

18. qui servat ficum comedet fructus eius et

sweetness of a man's friend by hearty counsel.

10 Thine own friend, and thy father's friend, forsake not; neither go into thy brother's house in the day of thy calamity: for better is a neighbour that is near than a brother far off.

11 My son, be wise, and make my heart glad, that I may answer him that reproacheth me.

12 A prudent man foreseeth the evil, and hideth himself; but the simple pass on, and are punished.

13 Take his garment that is surety for a stranger, and take a pledge of him for a strange woman.

14 He that blesseth his friend with a loud voice, rising early in the morning, it shall be counted a curse to him.

15 A continual dropping in a very rainy day and a contentious woman are alike.

16 Whosoever hideth her hideth the wind, and the ointment of his right hand, which bewrayeth itself.

17 Iron sharpeneth iron; so a man sharpeneth the countenance of his friend.

18 Whoso keepeth the fig

qui custos est domini sui glorificabitur

19. quomodo in aquis resplendent vultus prospicientium sic corda hominum manifesta sunt prudentibus

20. infernus et perditio non replentur similiter et oculi hominum insatiabiles

21. quomodo probatur in conflatorio argentum et in fornace aurum sic probatur homo ore laudantis

22. si contuderis stultum in pila quasi tisanas feriente desuper pilo non auferetur ab eo stultitia eius

23. diligenter agnosce vultum pecoris tui tuosque greges considera

24. non enim habebis iugiter potestatem sed corona tribuetur in generatione generationum

25. aperta sunt prata et apparuerunt herbae virentes et collecta sunt faena de montibus

26. agni ad vestimentum tuum et hedi agri pretium

27. sufficiat tibi lac caprarum in cibos tuos in

tree shall eat the fruit thereof: so he that waiteth on his master shall be honoured.

19 As in water face answereth to face, so the heart of man to man.

20 Hell and destruction are never full; so the eyes of man are never satisfied.

21 As the fining pot for silver, and the furnace for gold; so is a man to his praise.

22 Though thou shouldest bray a fool in a mortar among wheat with a pestle, yet will not his foolishness depart from him.

23 Be thou diligent to know the state of thy flocks, and look well to thy herds.

24 For riches are not for ever: and doth the crown endure to every generation?

25 The hay appeareth, and the tender grass sheweth itself, and herbs of the mountains are gathered.

26 The lambs are for thy clothing, and the goats are the price of the field.

27 And thou shalt have goats' milk enough for thy food, for the food of thy household, and for the maintenance for thy maidens.

necessaria domus tuae et
ad victum ancillis tuis

CHAPTER 28

1. fugit impius nemine
persequente iustus autem
quasi leo confidens
absque terrore erit
2. propter peccata terrae
multi principes eius et
propter hominis
sapientiam et horum
scientiam quae dicuntur
vita ducis longior erit
3. vir pauper calumnians
pauperes similis imbri
vehementi in quo paratur
fames
4. qui derelinquunt legem
laudant impium qui
custodiunt succenduntur
contra eum
5. viri mali non cogitant
iudicium qui autem
requirunt Dominum
animadvertunt omnia
6. melior est pauper
ambulans in simplicitate
sua quam dives pravis
itineribus
7. qui custodit legem
filius sapiens est qui
pascit comesatores
confundit patrem suum

CHAPTER 28

THE wicked flee when no
man pursueth: but the
righteous are bold as a lion.
2 For the transgression of a
land many are the princes
thereof: but by a man of
understanding and
knowledge the state thereof
shall be prolonged.
3 A poor man that oppresseth
the poor is like a sweeping
rain which leaveth no food.
4 They that forsake the law
praise the wicked: but such
as keep the law contend with
them.
5 Evil men understand not
judgment: but they that seek
the Lord understand all
things.
6 Better is the poor that
walketh in his uprightness,
than he that is perverse in his
ways, though he be rich.
7 Whoso keepeth the law is a
wise son: but he that is a
companion of riotous men
shameth his father.
8 He that by usury and unjust
gain increaseth his substance,

8. qui coacervat divitias usuris et fenore liberali in pauperes congregat eas

9. qui declinat aurem suam ne audiat legem oratio eius erit execrabilis

10. qui decipit iustos in via mala in interitu suo corruet et simplices possidebunt bona

11. sapiens sibi videtur vir dives pauper autem prudens scrutabitur eum

12. in exultatione iustorum multa gloria regnantibus impiis ruinae hominum

13. qui abscondit scelera sua non dirigetur qui confessus fuerit et reliquerit ea misericordiam consequetur

14. beatus homo qui semper est pavidus qui vero mentis est durae corruet in malum

15. leo rugiens et ursus esuriens princeps impius super populum pauperem

16. dux indigens prudentia multos opprimet per calumniam qui autem odit avaritiam longi fient dies eius

17. hominem qui

he shall gather it for him that will pity the poor.

9 He that turneth away his ear from hearing the law, even his prayer shall be abomination.

10 Whoso causeth the righteous to go astray in an evil way, he shall fall himself into his own pit: but the upright shall have good things in possession.

11 The rich man is wise in his own conceit; but the poor that hath understanding searcheth him out.

12 When righteous men do rejoice, there is great glory: but when the wicked rise, a man is hidden.

13 He that covereth his sins shall not prosper: but whoso confesseth and forsaketh them shall have mercy.

14 Happy is the man that feareth alway: but he that hardeneth his heart shall fall into mischief.

15 As a roaring lion, and a ranging bear; so is a wicked ruler over the poor people.

16 The prince that wanteth understanding is also a great oppressor: but he that hateth covetousness shall prolong his days.

calumniatur animae sanguinem si usque ad lacum fugerit nemo sustentet

18. qui ambulat simpliciter salvus erit qui perversis ingreditur viis concidet semel

19. qui operatur terram suam saturabitur panibus qui sectatur otium replebitur egestate

20. vir fidelis multum laudabitur qui autem festinat ditari non erit innocens

21. qui cognoscit in iudicio faciem non facit bene iste et pro buccella panis deserit veritatem

22. vir qui festinat ditari et aliis invidet ignorat quod egestas superveniat ei

23. qui corripit hominem gratiam postea inveniet apud eum magis quam ille qui per linguae blandimenta decipit

24. qui subtrahit aliquid a patre suo et matre et dicit hoc non est peccatum particeps homicidae est

25. qui se iactat et dilatat iurgia concitat qui sperat in Domino saginabitur

17 A man that doeth violence to the blood of any person shall flee to the pit; let no man stay him.

18 Whoso walketh uprightly shall be saved: but he that is perverse in his ways shall fall at once.

19 He that tilleth his land shall have plenty of bread: but he that followeth after vain persons shall have poverty enough.

20 A faithful man shall abound with blessings: but he that maketh haste to be rich shall not be innocent.

21 To have respect of persons is not good: for for a piece of bread that man will transgress.

22 He that hasteth to be rich hath an evil eye, and considereth not that poverty shall come upon him.

23 He that rebuketh a man afterwards shall find more favour than he that flattereth with the tongue.

24 Whoso robbeth his father or his mother, and saith, It is no transgression; the same is the companion of a destroyer.

25 He that is of a proud heart stirreth up strife: but he that

26. qui confidit in corde suo stultus est qui autem graditur sapienter iste salvabitur

27. qui dat pauperi non indigebit qui despicit deprecantem sustinebit penuriam

28. cum surrexerint impii abscondentur homines cum illi perierint multiplicabuntur iusti

putteth his trust in the Lord shall be made fat.

26 He that trusteth in his own heart is a fool: but whoso walketh wisely, he shall be delivered.

27 He that giveth unto the poor shall not lack: but he that hideth his eyes shall have many a curse.

28 When the wicked rise, men hide themselves: but when they perish, the righteous increase.

CHAPTER 29

1. viro qui corripientem dura cervice contemnit repentinus superveniet interitus et eum sanitas non sequitur

2. in multiplicatione iustorum laetabitur vulgus cum impii sumpserint principatum gemet populus

3. vir qui amat sapientiam laetificat patrem suum qui autem nutrit scorta perdet substantiam

4. rex iustus erigit terram vir avarus destruet eam

5. homo qui blandis fictisque sermonibus

CHAPTER 29

HE, that being often reproved hardeneth his neck, shall suddenly be destroyed, and that without remedy.

2 When the righteous are in authority, the people rejoice: but when the wicked beareth rule, the people mourn.

3 Whoso loveth wisdom rejoiceth his father: but he that keepeth company with harlots spendeth his substance.

4 The king by judgment establisheth the land: but he that receiveth gifts overthroweth it.

5 A man that flattereth his

loquitur amico suo rete expandit gressibus eius

6. peccantem virum iniquum involvet laqueus et iustus laudabit atque gaudebit

7. novit iustus causam pauperum impius ignorat scientiam

8. homines pestilentes dissipant civitatem sapientes avertunt furorem

9. vir sapiens si cum stulto contenderit sive irascatur sive rideat non inveniet requiem

10. viri sanguinum oderunt simplicem iusti quaerunt animam eius

11. totum spiritum suum profert stultus sapiens differt et reservat in posterum

12. princeps qui libenter audit verba mendacii omnes ministros habebit impios

13. pauper et creditor obviam fuerunt sibi utriusque inluminator est Dominus

14. rex qui iudicat in veritate pauperes thronus eius in aeternum firmabitur

neighbour spreadeth a net for his feet.

6 In the transgression of an evil man there is a snare: but the righteous doth sing and rejoice.

7 The righteous considereth the cause of the poor: but the wicked regardeth not to know it.

8 Scornful men bring a city into a snare: but wise men turn away wrath.

9 If a wise man contendeth with a foolish man, whether he rage or laugh, there is no rest.

10 The bloodthirsty hate the upright: but the just seek his soul.

11 A fool uttereth all his mind: but a wise man keepeth it in till afterwards.

12 If a ruler hearken to lies, all his servants are wicked.

13 The poor and the deceitful man meet together: the Lord lighteneth both their eyes.

14 The king that faithfully judgeth the poor, his throne shall be established for ever.

15 The rod and reproof give wisdom: but a child left to himself bringeth his mother to shame.

16 When the wicked are

15. virga atque correptio tribuet sapientiam puer autem qui dimittitur voluntati suae confundet matrem suam

16. in multiplicatione impiorum multiplicabuntur scelera et iusti ruinas eorum videbunt

17. erudi filium tuum et refrigerabit te et dabit delicias animae tuae

18. cum prophetia defecerit dissipabitur populus qui custodit legem beatus est

19. servus verbis non potest erudiri quia quod dicis intellegit et respondere contemnit

20. vidisti hominem velocem ad loquendum stulti magis speranda est quam illius correptio

21. qui delicate a pueritia nutrit servum suum postea illum sentiet contumacem

22. vir iracundus provocat rixas et qui ad indignandum facilis est erit ad peccata proclivior

23. superbum sequitur humilitas et humilem spiritu suscipiet gloria

multiplied, transgression increaseth: but the righteous shall see their fall.

17 Correct thy son, and he shall give thee rest; yea, he shall give delight unto thy soul.

18 Where there is no vision, the people perish: but he that keepeth the law, happy is he.

19 A servant will not be corrected by words: for though he understand he will not answer.

20 Seest thou a man that is hasty in his words? there is more hope of a fool than of him.

21 He that delicately bringeth up his servant from a child shall have him become his son at the length.

22 An angry man stirreth up strife, and a furious man aboundeth in transgression.

23 A man's pride shall bring him low: but honour shall uphold the humble in spirit.

24 Whoso is partner with a thief hateth his own soul: he heareth cursing, and bewrayeth it not.

25 The fear of man bringeth a snare: but whoso putteth his trust in the Lord shall be safe.

24. qui cum fure partitur odit animam suam adiurantem audit et non indicat

25. qui timet hominem cito corruet qui sperat in Domino sublevabitur

26. multi requirunt faciem principis et a Domino iudicium egreditur singulorum

27. abominantur iusti virum impium et abominantur impii eos qui in recta sunt via

26 Many seek the ruler's favour; but every man's judgment cometh from the Lord.

27 An unjust man is an abomination to the just: and he that is upright in the way is abomination to the wicked.

CHAPTER 30

1. verba Congregantis filii Vomentis visio quam locutus est vir cum quo est Deus et qui Deo secum morante confortatus ait

2. stultissimus sum virorum et sapientia hominum non est mecum

3. non didici sapientiam et non novi sanctorum scientiam

4. quis ascendit in caelum atque descendit quis continuit spiritum manibus suis quis conligavit aquas quasi in

CHAPTER 30

THE words of Agur the son of Jakeh, even the prophecy: the man spake unto Ithiel, even unto Ithiel and Ucal,

2 Surely I am more brutish than any man, and have not the understanding of a man.

3 I neither learned wisdom, nor have the knowledge of the holy.

4 Who hath ascended up into heaven, or descended? who hath gathered the wind in his fists? who hath bound the waters in a garment? who hath established all the ends of the earth? what is his

vestimento quis suscitavit omnes terminos terrae quod nomen eius et quod nomen filii eius si nosti

5. omnis sermo Dei ignitus clypeus est sperantibus in se

6. ne addas quicquam verbis illius et arguaris inveniarisque mendax

7. duo rogavi te ne deneges mihi antequam moriar

8. vanitatem et verba mendacia longe fac a me mendicitatem et divitias ne dederis mihi tribue tantum victui meo necessaria

9. ne forte saturatus inliciar ad negandum et dicam quis est Dominus et egestate conpulsus furer et peierem nomen Dei mei

10. ne accuses servum ad dominum suum ne forte maledicat tibi et corruas

11. generatio quae patri suo maledicit et quae non benedicit matri suae

12. generatio quae sibi munda videtur et tamen non est lota a sordibus suis

13. generatio cuius

name, and what is his son's name, if thou canst tell?

5 Every word of God is pure: he is a shield unto them that put their trust in him.

6 Add thou not unto his words, lest he reprove thee, and thou be found a liar.

7 Two things have I required of thee; deny me them not before I die:

8 Remove far from me vanity and lies: give me neither poverty nor riches; feed me with food convenient for me:

9 Lest I be full, and deny thee, and say, Who is the Lord? or lest I be poor, and steal, and take the name of my God in vain.

10 Accuse not a servant unto his master, lest he curse thee, and thou be found guilty.

11 There is a generation that curseth their father, and doth not bless their mother.

12 There is a generation that are pure in their own eyes, and yet is not washed from their filthiness.

13 There is a generation, O how lofty are their eyes! and their eyelids are lifted up.

14 There is a generation, whose teeth are as swords, and their jaw teeth as knives,

excelsi sunt oculi et palpebrae eius in alta subrectae

14. generatio quae pro dentibus gladios habet et commandit molaribus suis ut comedat inopes de terra et pauperes ex hominibus

15. sanguisugae duae sunt filiae dicentes adfer adfer tria sunt insaturabilia et quartum quod numquam dicit sufficit

16. infernus et os vulvae et terra quae non satiatur aqua ignis vero numquam dicit sufficit

17. oculum qui subsannat patrem et qui despicit partum matris suae effodiant corvi de torrentibus et comedant illum filii aquilae

18. tria sunt difficilia mihi et quartum penitus ignoro

19. viam aquilae in caelo viam colubri super petram viam navis in medio mari et viam viri in adulescentula

20. talis est via mulieris adulterae quae comedit et tergens os suum dicit non sum operata malum

to devour the poor from off the earth, and the needy from among men.

15 The horseleach hath two daughters, crying, Give, give. There are three things that are never satisfied, yea, four things say not, It is enough:

16 The grave; and the barren womb; the earth that is not filled with water; and the fire that saith not, It is enough.

17 The eye that mocketh at his father, and despiseth to obey his mother, the ravens of the valley shall pick it out, and the young eagles shall eat it.

18 There be three things which are too wonderful for me, yea, four which I know not:

19 The way of an eagle in the air; the way of a serpent upon a rock; the way of a ship in the midst of the sea; and the way of a man with a maid.

20 Such is the way of an adulterous woman; she eateth, and wipeth her mouth, and saith, I have done no wickedness.

21 For three things the earth is disquieted, and for four which it cannot bear:

22 For a servant when he

21. per tria movetur terra et quartum non potest sustinere

22. per servum cum regnaverit per stultum cum saturatus fuerit cibo

23. per odiosam mulierem cum in matrimonio fuerit adsumpta et per ancillam cum heres fuerit dominae suae

24. quattuor sunt minima terrae et ipsa sunt sapientiora sapientibus

25. formicae populus infirmus quae praeparant in messe cibum sibi

26. lepusculus plebs invalida quae conlocat in petra cubile suum

27. regem lucusta non habet et egreditur universa per turmas

28. stilio manibus nititur et moratur in aedibus regis

29. tria sunt quae bene gradiuntur et quartum quod incedit feliciter

30. leo fortissimus bestiarum ad nullius pavebit occursum

31. gallus succinctus lumbos et aries nec est rex qui resistat ei

reigneth; and a fool when he is filled with meat;

23 For an odious woman when she is married; and an handmaid that is heir to her mistress.

24 There be four things which are little upon the earth, but they are exceeding wise:

25 The ants are a people not strong, yet they prepare their meat in the summer;

26 The conies are but a feeble folk, yet make they their houses in the rocks;

27 The locusts have no king, yet go they forth all of them by bands;

28 The spider taketh hold with her hands, and is in kings' palaces.

29 There be three things which go well, yea, four are comely in going:

30 A lion which is strongest among beasts, and turneth not away for any;

31 A greyhound; an he goat also; and a king, against whom there is no rising up.

32 If thou hast done foolishly in lifting up thyself, or if thou hast thought evil, lay thine hand upon thy mouth.

33 Surely the churning of

32. et qui stultus apparuit postquam elatus est in sublime si enim intellexisset ori inposuisset manum

33. qui autem fortiter premit ubera ad eliciendum lac exprimit butyrum et qui vehementer emungitur elicit sanguinem et qui provocat iras producit discordias

milk bringeth forth butter, and the wringing of the nose bringeth forth blood: so the forcing of wrath bringeth forth strife.

CHAPTER 31

1. verba Lamuhel regis visio qua erudivit eum mater sua

2. quid dilecte mi quid dilecte uteri mei quid dilecte votorum meorum

3. ne dederis mulieribus substantiam tuam et vias tuas ad delendos reges

4. noli regibus o Lamuhel noli regibus dare vinum quia nullum secretum est ubi regnat ebrietas

5. ne forte bibat et obliviscatur iudiciorum et mutet causam filiorum pauperis

6. date siceram maerentibus et vinum his

CHAPTER 31

THE words of king Lemuel, the prophecy that his mother taught him.

2 What, my son? and what, the son of my womb? and what, the son of my vows?

3 Give not thy strength unto women, nor thy ways to that which destroyeth kings.

4 It is not for kings, O Lemuel, it is not for kings to drink wine; nor for princes strong drink:

5 Lest they drink, and forget the law, and pervert the judgment of any of the afflicted.

6 Give strong drink unto him that is ready to perish, and

qui amaro sunt animo

7. bibant ut obliviscantur egestatis suae et doloris non recordentur amplius

8. aperi os tuum muto et causis omnium filiorum qui pertranseunt

9. aperi os tuum decerne quod iustum est et iudica inopem et pauperem

10. aleph mulierem fortem quis inveniet procul et de ultimis finibus pretium eius

11. beth confidit in ea cor viri sui et spoliis non indigebit

12. gimel reddet ei bonum et non malum omnibus diebus vitae suae

13. deleth quaesivit lanam et linum et operata est consilio manuum suarum

14. he facta est quasi navis institoris de longe portat panem suum

15. vav et de nocte surrexit deditque praedam domesticis suis et cibaria ancillis suis

16. zai consideravit agrum et emit eum de fructu manuum suarum plantavit vineam

wine unto those that be of heavy hearts.

7 Let him drink, and forget his poverty, and remember his misery no more.

8 Open thy mouth for the dumb in the cause of all such as are appointed to destruction.

9 Open thy mouth, judge righteously, and plead the cause of the poor and needy.

10 Who can find a virtuous woman? for her price is far above rubies.

11 The heart of her husband doth safely trust in her, so that he shall have no need of spoil.

12 She will do him good and not evil all the days of her life.

13 She seeketh wool, and flax, and worketh willingly with her hands.

14 She is like the merchants' ships; she bringeth her food from afar.

15 She riseth also while it is yet night, and giveth meat to her household, and a portion to her maidens.

16 She considereth a field, and buyeth it: with the fruit of her hands she planteth a vineyard.

17. heth accinxit fortitudine lumbos suos et roboravit brachium suum

18. teth gustavit quia bona est negotiatio eius non extinguetur in nocte lucerna illius

19. ioth manum suam misit ad fortia et digiti eius adprehenderunt fusum

20. caph manum suam aperuit inopi et palmas suas extendit ad pauperem

21. lameth non timebit domui suae a frigoribus nivis omnes enim domestici eius vestiti duplicibus

22. mem stragulam vestem fecit sibi byssus et purpura indumentum eius

23. nun nobilis in portis vir eius quando sederit cum senatoribus terrae

24. samech sindonem fecit et vendidit et cingulum tradidit Chananeo

25. ain fortitudo et decor indumentum eius et ridebit in die novissimo

26. phe os suum aperuit sapientiae et lex clementiae in lingua eius

17 She girdeth her loins with strength, and strengtheneth her arms.

18 She perceiveth that her merchandise is good: her candle goeth not out by night.

19 She layeth her hands to the spindle, and her hands hold the distaff.

20 She stretcheth out her hand to the poor; yea, she reacheth forth her hands to the needy.

21 She is not afraid of the snow for her household: for all her household are clothed with scarlet.

22 She maketh herself coverings of tapestry; her clothing is silk and purple.

23 Her husband is known in the gates, when he sitteth among the elders of the land.

24 She maketh fine linen, and selleth it; and delivereth girdles unto the merchant.

25 Strength and honour are her clothing; and she shall rejoice in time to come.

26 She openeth her mouth with wisdom; and in her tongue is the law of kindness.

27 She looketh well to the ways of her household, and eateth not the bread of

27. sade considerat semitas domus suae et panem otiosa non comedet

28. coph surrexerunt filii eius et beatissimam praedicaverunt vir eius et laudavit eam

29. res multae filiae congregaverunt divitias tu supergressa es universas

30. sin fallax gratia et vana est pulchritudo mulier timens Dominum ipsa laudabitur

31. thau date ei de fructu manuum suarum et laudent eam in portis opera eius

idleness.

28 Her children arise up, and call her blessed; her husband also, and he praiseth her.

29 Many daughters have done virtuously, but thou excellest them all.

30 Favour is deceitful, and beauty is vain: but a woman that feareth the Lord, she shall be praised.

31 Give her of the fruit of her hands; and let her own works praise her in the gates.

ECCLESIASTES,
or THE PRACHER

ECCLESIASTES,
or THE PREACHER

CHAPTER 1

1. verba Ecclesiastes filii David regis Hierusalem
2. vanitas vanitatum dixit Ecclesiastes vanitas vanitatum omnia vanitas
3. quid habet amplius homo de universo labore suo quod laborat sub sole
4. generatio praeterit et generatio advenit terra vero in aeternum stat
5. oritur sol et occidit et ad locum suum revertitur ibique renascens
6. gyrat per meridiem et flectitur ad aquilonem lustrans universa circuitu pergit spiritus et in circulos suos regreditur
7. omnia flumina intrant mare et mare non redundat ad locum unde exeunt flumina revertuntur ut iterum fluant
8. cunctae res difficiles non potest eas homo explicare sermone non saturatur oculus visu nec

CHAPTER 1

THE words of the Preacher, the son of David, king in Jerusalem.

2 Vanity of vanities, saith the Preacher, vanity of vanities; all is vanity.

3 What profit hath a man of all his labour which he taketh under the sun?

4 One generation passeth away, and another generation cometh: but the earth abideth for ever.

5 The sun also ariseth, and the sun goeth down, and hasteth to his place where he arose.

6 The wind goeth toward the south, and turneth about unto the north; it whirleth about continually, and the wind returneth again according to his circuits.

7 All the rivers run into the sea; yet the sea is not full; unto the place from whence the rivers come, thither they return again.

8 All things are full of

auris impletur auditu

9. quid est quod fuit ipsum quod futurum est quid est quod factum est ipsum quod fiendum est

10. nihil sub sole novum nec valet quisquam dicere ecce hoc recens est iam enim praecessit in saeculis quae fuerunt ante nos

11. non est priorum memoria sed nec eorum quidem quae postea futura sunt erit recordatio apud eos qui futuri sunt in novissimo

12. ego Ecclesiastes fui rex Israhel in Hierusalem

13. et proposui in animo meo quaerere et investigare sapienter de omnibus quae fiunt sub sole hanc occupationem pessimam dedit Deus filiis hominum ut occuparentur in ea

14. vidi quae fiunt cuncta sub sole et ecce universa vanitas et adflictio spiritus

15. perversi difficile corriguntur et stultorum infinitus est numerus

16. locutus sum in corde meo dicens ecce magnus

labour; man cannot utter it: the eye is not satisfied with seeing, nor the ear filled with hearing.

9 The thing that hath been, it is that which shall be; and that which is done is that which shall be done: and there is no new thing under the sun.

10 Is there any thing whereof it may be said, See, this is new? it hath been already of old time, which was before us.

11 There is no remembrance of former things; neither shall there be any remembrance of things that are to come with those that shall come after.

12 I the Preacher was king over Israel in Jerusalem.

13 And I gave my heart to seek and search out by wisdom concerning all things that are done under heaven: this sore travail hath God given to the sons of man to be exercised therewith.

14 I have seen all the works that are done under the sun; and, behold, all is vanity and vexation of spirit.

15 That which is crooked cannot be made straight: and

effectus sum et praecessi sapientia omnes qui fuerunt ante me in Hierusalem et mens mea contemplata est multa sapienter et didicit

17. dedique cor meum ut scirem prudentiam atque doctrinam erroresque et stultitiam et agnovi quod in his quoque esset labor et adflictio spiritus

18. eo quod in multa sapientia multa sit indignatio et qui addit scientiam addat et laborem

that which is wanting cannot be numbered.

16 I communed with mine own heart, saying, Lo, I am come to great estate, and have gotten more wisdom than all they that have been before me in Jerusalem: yea, my heart had great experience of wisdom and knowledge.

17 And I gave my heart to know wisdom, and to know madness and folly: I perceived that this also is vexation of spirit.

18 For in much wisdom is much grief: and he that increaseth knowledge increaseth sorrow.

CHAPTER 2

1. dixi ego in corde meo vadam et affluam deliciis et fruar bonis et vidi quod hoc quoque esset vanitas

2. risum reputavi errorem et gaudio dixi quid frustra deciperis

3. cogitavi in corde meo abstrahere a vino carnem meam ut animum meum transferrem ad sapientiam devitaremque stultitiam

CHAPTER 2

I SAID in mine heart, Go to now, I will prove thee with mirth, therefore enjoy pleasure: and, behold, this also is vanity.

2 I said of laughter, It is mad: and of mirth, What doeth it?

3 I sought in mine heart to give myself unto wine, yet acquainting mine heart with wisdom; and to lay hold on folly, till I might see what

donec viderem quid esset utile filiis hominum quod facto opus est sub sole numero dierum vitae suae

4. magnificavi opera mea aedificavi mihi domos plantavi vineas

5. feci hortos et pomeria et consevi ea cuncti generis arboribus

6. extruxi mihi piscinas aquarum ut inrigarem silvam lignorum germinantium

7. possedi servos et ancillas multamque familiam habui armenta quoque et magnos ovium greges ultra omnes qui fuerunt ante me in Hierusalem

8. coacervavi mihi argentum et aurum et substantias regum ac provinciarum feci mihi cantores et cantrices et delicias filiorum hominum scyphos et urceos in ministerio ad vina fundenda

9. et supergressus sum opibus omnes qui fuerunt ante me in Hierusalem sapientia quoque perseveravit mecum

10. et omnia quae

was that good for the sons of men, which they should do under the heaven all the days of their life.

4 I made me great works; I builded me houses; I planted me vineyards:

5 I made me gardens and orchards, and I planted trees in them of all kind of fruits:

6 I made me pools of water, to water therewith the wood that bringeth forth trees:

7 I got me servants and maidens, and had servants born in my house; also I had great possessions of great and small cattle above all that were in Jerusalem before me:

8 I gathered me also silver and gold, and the peculiar treasure of kings and of the provinces: I gat me men singers and women singers, and the delights of the sons of men, as musical instruments, and that of all sorts.

9 So I was great, and increased more than all that were before me in Jerusalem: also my wisdom remained with me.

10 And whatsoever mine eyes desired I kept not from

desideraverunt oculi mei non negavi eis nec prohibui cor quin omni voluptate frueretur et oblectaret se in his quae paraveram et hanc ratus sum partem meam si uterer labore meo

11. cumque me convertissem ad universa opera quae fecerant manus meae et ad labores in quibus frustra sudaveram vidi in omnibus vanitatem et adflictionem animi et nihil permanere sub sole

12. transivi ad contemplandam sapientiam erroresque et stultitiam quid est inquam homo ut sequi possit regem factorem suum

13. et vidi quia tantum praecederet sapientia stultitiam quantum differt lux tenebris

14. sapientis oculi in capite eius stultus in tenebris ambulat et didici quod unus utriusque esset interitus

15. et dixi in corde meo si unus et stulti et meus occasus erit quid mihi prodest quod maiorem

them, I withheld not my heart from any joy; for my heart rejoiced in all my labour: and this was my portion of all my labour.

11 Then I looked on all the works that my hands had wrought, and on the labour that I had laboured to do: and, behold, all was vanity and vexation of spirit, and there was no profit under the sun.

12 And I turned myself to behold wisdom, and madness, and folly: for what can the man do that cometh after the king? even that which hath been already done.

13 Then I saw that wisdom excelleth folly, as far as light excelleth darkness.

14 The wise man's eyes are in his head; but the fool walketh in darkness: and I myself perceived also that one event happeneth to them all.

15 Then said I in my heart, As it happeneth to the fool, so it happeneth even to me; and why was I then more wise? Then I said in my heart, that this also is vanity.

16 For there is no

sapientiae dedi operam locutusque cum mente mea animadverti quod hoc quoque esset vanitas

16. non enim erit memoria sapientis similiter ut stulti in perpetuum et futura tempora oblivione cuncta pariter obruent moritur doctus similiter et indoctus

17. et idcirco taeduit me vitae meae videntem mala esse universa sub sole et cuncta vanitatem atque adflictionem spiritus

18. rursum detestatus sum omnem industriam meam quae sub sole studiosissime laboravi habiturus heredem post me

19. quem ignoro utrum sapiens an stultus futurus sit et dominabitur in laboribus meis quibus desudavi et sollicitus fui et est quicquam tam vanum

20. unde cessavi renuntiavitque cor meum ultra laborare sub sole

21. nam cum alius laboret in sapientia et doctrina et

remembrance of the wise more than of the fool for ever; seeing that which now is in the days to come shall all be forgotten. And how dieth the wise man? as the fool.

17 Therefore I hated life; because the work that is wrought under the sun is grievous unto me: for all is vanity and vexation of spirit.

18 Yea, I hated all my labour which I had taken under the sun: because I should leave it unto the man that shall be after me.

19 And who knoweth whether he shall be a wise man or a fool? yet shall he have rule over all my labour wherein I have laboured, and wherein I have shewed myself wise under the sun. This is also vanity.

20 Therefore I went about to cause my heart to despair of all the labour which I took under the sun.

21 For there is a man whose labour is in wisdom, and in knowledge, and in equity; yet to a man that hath not laboured therein shall he leave it for his portion. This also is vanity and a great

sollicitudine homini otioso quaesita dimittit et hoc ergo vanitas et magnum malum

22. quid enim proderit homini de universo labore suo et adflictione spiritus qua sub sole cruciatus est

23. cuncti dies eius doloribus et aerumnis pleni sunt nec per noctem mente requiescit et haec non vanitas est

24. nonne melius est comedere et bibere et ostendere animae suae bona de laboribus suis et hoc de manu Dei est

25. quis ita vorabit et deliciis affluet ut ego

26. homini bono in conspectu suo dedit Deus sapientiam et scientiam et laetitiam peccatori autem dedit adflictionem et curam superfluam ut addat et congreget et tradat ei qui placuit Deo sed et hoc vanitas et cassa sollicitudo mentis

evil.

22 For what hath man of all his labour, and of the vexation of his heart, wherein he hath laboured under the sun?

23 For all his days are sorrows, and his travail grief; yea, his heart taketh not rest in the night. This is also vanity.

24 There is nothing better for a man, than that he should eat and drink, and that he should make his soul enjoy good in his labour. This also I saw, that it was from the hand of God.

25 For who can eat, or who else can hasten hereunto, more than I?

26 For God giveth to a man that is good in his sight wisdom, and knowledge, and joy: but to the sinner he giveth travail, to gather and to heap up, that he may give to him that is good before God. This also is vanity and vexation of spirit.

CHAPTER 3

1. omnia tempus habent et suis spatiis transeunt universa sub caelo

2. tempus nascendi et tempus moriendi tempus plantandi et tempus evellendi quod plantatum est

3. tempus occidendi et tempus sanandi tempus destruendi et tempus aedificandi

4. tempus flendi et tempus ridendi tempus plangendi et tempus saltandi

5. tempus spargendi lapides et tempus colligendi tempus amplexandi et tempus longe fieri a conplexibus

6. tempus adquirendi et tempus perdendi tempus custodiendi et tempus abiciendi

7. tempus scindendi et tempus consuendi tempus tacendi et tempus loquendi

8. tempus dilectionis et tempus odii tempus belli et tempus pacis

9. quid habet amplius

TO every thing there is a season, and a time to every purpose under the heaven:

2 A time to be born, and a time to die; a time to plant, and a time to pluck up that which is planted;

3 A time to kill, and a time to heal; a time to break down, and a time to build up;

4 A time to weep, and a time to laugh; a time to mourn, and a time to dance;

5 A time to cast away stones, and a time to gather stones together; a time to embrace, and a time to refrain from embracing;

6 A time to get, and a time to lose; a time to keep, and a time to cast away;

7 A time to rend, and a time to sew; a time to keep silence, and a time to speak;

8 A time to love, and a time to hate; a time of war, and a time of peace.

9 What profit hath he that worketh in that wherein he laboureth?

10 I have seen the travail, which God hath given to the sons of men to be exercised

homo de labore suo

10. vidi adflictionem quam dedit Deus filiis hominum ut distendantur in ea

11. cuncta fecit bona in tempore suo et mundum tradidit disputationi eorum ut non inveniat homo opus quod operatus est Deus ab initio usque ad finem

12. et cognovi quod non esset melius nisi laetari et facere bene in vita sua

13. omnis enim homo qui comedit et bibit et videt bonum de labore suo hoc donum Dei est

14. didici quod omnia opera quae fecit Deus perseverent in perpetuum non possumus eis quicquam addere nec auferre quae fecit Deus ut timeatur

15. quod factum est ipsum permanet quae futura sunt iam fuerunt et Deus instaurat quod abiit

16. vidi sub sole in loco iudicii impietatem et in loco iustitiae iniquitatem

17. et dixi in corde meo iustum et impium iudicabit Deus et tempus

in it.

11 He hath made every thing beautiful in his time: also he hath set the world in their heart, so that no man can find out the work that God maketh from the beginning to the end.

12 I know that there is no good in them, but for a man to rejoice, and to do good in his life.

13 And also that every man should eat and drink, and enjoy the good of all his labour, it is the gift of God.

14 I know that, whatsoever God doeth, it shall be for ever: nothing can be put to it, nor any thing taken from it: and God doeth it, that men should fear before him.

15 That which hath been is now; and that which is to be hath already been; and God requireth that which is past.

16 And moreover I saw under the sun the place of judgment, that wickedness was there; and the place of righteousness, that iniquity was there.

17 I said in mine heart, God shall judge the righteous and the wicked: for there is a time there for every purpose

109

omni rei tunc erit

18. dixi in corde meo de filiis hominum ut probaret eos Deus et ostenderet similes esse bestiis

19. idcirco unus interitus est hominis et iumentorum et aequa utriusque condicio sicut moritur homo sic et illa moriuntur similiter spirant omnia et nihil habet homo iumento amplius cuncta subiacent vanitati

20. et omnia pergunt ad unum locum de terra facta sunt et in terram pariter revertentur

21. quis novit si spiritus filiorum Adam ascendat sursum et si spiritus iumentorum descendat deorsum

22. et deprehendi nihil esse melius quam laetari hominem in opere suo et hanc esse partem illius quis enim eum adducet ut post se futura cognoscat

and for every work.

18 I said in mine heart concerning the estate of the sons of men, that God might manifest them, and that they might see that they themselves are beasts.

19 For that which befalleth the sons of men befalleth beasts; even one thing befalleth them: as the one dieth, so dieth the other; yea, they have all one breath; so that a man hath no preeminence above a beast: for all is vanity.

20 All go unto one place; all are of the dust, and all turn to dust again.

21 Who knoweth the spirit of man that goeth upward, and the spirit of the beast that goeth downward to the earth?

22 Wherefore I perceive that there is nothing better, than that a man should rejoice in his own works; for that is his portion: for who shall bring him to see what shall be after him?

CHAPTER 4

1. verti me ad alia et vidi calumnias quae sub sole geruntur et lacrimas innocentum et consolatorem neminem nec posse resistere eorum violentiae cunctorum auxilio destitutos

2. et laudavi magis mortuos quam viventes

3. et feliciorem utroque iudicavi qui necdum natus est nec vidit mala quae sub sole fiunt

4. rursum contemplatus omnes labores hominum et industrias animadverti patere invidiae proximi et in hoc ergo vanitas et cura superflua est

5. stultus conplicat manus suas et comedit carnes suas dicens

6. melior est pugillus cum requie quam plena utraque manus cum labore et adflictione animi

7. considerans repperi et aliam vanitatem sub sole

8. unus est et secundum non habet non filium non fratrem et tamen laborare

CHAPTER 4

SO I returned, and considered all the oppressions that are done under the sun: and behold the tears of such as were oppressed, and they had no comforter; and on the side of their oppressors there was power; but they had no comforter.

2 Wherefore I praised the dead which are already dead more than the living which are yet alive.

3 Yea, better is he than both they, which hath not yet been, who hath not seen the evil work that is done under the sun.

4 Again, I considered all travail, and every right work, that for this a man is envied of his neighbour. This is also vanity and vexation of spirit.

5 The fool foldeth his hands together, and eateth his own flesh.

6 Better is an handful with quietness, than both the hands full with travail and vexation of spirit.

7 Then I returned, and I saw vanity under the sun.

111

non cessat nec satiantur oculi eius divitiis nec recogitat dicens cui laboro et fraudo animam meam bonis in hoc quoque vanitas est et adflictio pessima

9. melius ergo est duos simul esse quam unum habent enim emolumentum societatis suae

10. si unus ceciderit ab altero fulcietur vae soli quia cum ruerit non habet sublevantem

11. et si dormierint duo fovebuntur mutuo unus quomodo calefiet

12. et si quispiam praevaluerit contra unum duo resistent ei funiculus triplex difficile rumpitur

13. melior est puer pauper et sapiens rege sene et stulto qui nescit providere in posterum

14. quod et de carcere catenisque interdum quis egrediatur ad regnum et alius natus in regno inopia consumatur

15. vidi cunctos viventes qui ambulant sub sole cum adulescente secundo qui consurgit pro eo

8 There is one alone, and there is not a second; yea, he hath neither child nor brother: yet is there no end of all his labour; neither is his eye satisfied with riches; neither saith he, For whom do I labour, and bereave my soul of good? This is also vanity, yea, it is a sore travail.

9 Two are better than one; because they have a good reward for their labour.

10 For if they fall, the one will lift up his fellow: but woe to him that is alone when he falleth; for he hath not another to help him up.

11 Again, if two lie together, then they have heat: but how can one be warm alone?

12 And if one prevail against him, two shall withstand him; and a threefold cord is not quickly broken.

13 Better is a poor and a wise child than an old and foolish king, who will no more be admonished.

14 For out of prison he cometh to reign; whereas also he that is born in his kingdom becometh poor.

15 I considered all the living which walk under the sun,

16. infinitus numerus est populi omnium qui fuerunt ante eum et qui postea futuri sunt non laetabuntur in eo sed et hoc vanitas et adflictio spiritus

17. custodi pedem tuum ingrediens domum Dei multo enim melior est oboedientia quam stultorum victimae qui nesciunt quid faciant mali

with the second child that shall stand up in his stead.

16 There is no end of all the people, even of all that have been before them: they also that come after shall not rejoice in him. Surely this also is vanity and vexation of spirit.

CHAPTER 5

1. ne temere quid loquaris neque cor tuum sit velox ad proferendum sermonem coram Deo Deus enim in caelo et tu super terram idcirco sint pauci sermones tui

2. multas curas sequuntur somnia et in multis sermonibus invenitur stultitia

3. si quid vovisti Deo ne moreris reddere displicet enim ei infidelis et stulta promissio sed quodcumque voveris redde

4. multoque melius est non vovere quam post

CHAPTER 5

KEEP thy foot when thou goest to the house of God, and be more ready to hear, than to give the sacrifice of fools: for they consider not that they do evil.

2 Be not rash with thy mouth, and let not thine heart be hasty to utter any thing before God: for God is in heaven, and thou upon earth: therefore let thy words be few.

3 For a dream cometh through the multitude of business; and a fool's voice is known by multitude of words.

4 When thou vowest a vow

113

votum promissa non conplere

5. ne dederis os tuum ut peccare faciat carnem tuam neque dicas coram angelo non est providentia ne forte iratus Deus super sermone tuo dissipet cuncta opera manuum tuarum

6. ubi multa sunt somnia plurimae vanitates et sermones innumeri tu vero Deum time

7. si videris calumnias egenorum et violenta iudicia et subverti iustitiam in provincia non mireris super hoc negotio quia excelso alius excelsior est et super hos quoque eminentiores sunt alii

8. et insuper universae terrae rex imperat servienti

9. avarus non implebitur pecunia et qui amat divitias fructus non capiet ex eis et hoc ergo vanitas

10. ubi multae sunt opes multi et qui comedant eas et quid prodest possessori nisi quod cernit divitias oculis suis

11. dulcis est somnus

unto God, defer not to pay it; for he hath no pleasure in fools: pay that which thou hast vowed.

5 Better is it that thou shouldest not vow, than that thou shouldest vow and not pay.

6 Suffer not thy mouth to cause thy flesh to sin; neither say thou before the angel, that it was an error: wherefore should God be angry at thy voice, and destroy the work of thine hands?

7 For in the multitude of dreams and many words there are also divers vanities: but fear thou God.

8 If thou seest the oppression of the poor, and violent perverting of judgment and justice in a province, marvel not at the matter: for he that is higher than the highest regardeth; and there be higher than they.

9 Moreover the profit of the earth is for all: the king himself is served by the field.

10 He that loveth silver shall not be satisfied with silver; nor he that loveth abundance with increase: this is also vanity.

operanti sive parum sive multum comedat saturitas autem divitis non sinit dormire eum

12. est et alia infirmitas pessima quam vidi sub sole divitiae conservatae in malum domini sui

13. pereunt enim in adflictione pessima generavit filium qui in summa egestate erit

14. sicut egressus est nudus de utero matris suae sic revertetur et nihil auferet secum de labore suo

15. miserabilis prorsus infirmitas quomodo venit sic revertetur quid ergo prodest ei quod laboravit in ventum

16. cunctis diebus vitae suae comedit in tenebris et in curis multis et in aerumna atque tristitia

17. hoc itaque mihi visum est bonum ut comedat quis et bibat et fruatur laetitia ex labore suo quod laboravit ipse sub sole numerum dierum vitae suae quos dedit ei Deus et haec est pars illius

18. et omni homini cui

11 When goods increase, they are increased that eat them: and what good is there to the owners thereof, saving the beholding of them with their eyes?

12 The sleep of a labouring man is sweet, whether he eat little or much: but the abundance of the rich will not suffer him to sleep.

13 There is a sore evil which I have seen under the sun, namely, riches kept for the owners thereof to their hurt.

14 But those riches perish by evil travail: and he begetteth a son, and there is nothing in his hand.

15 As he came forth of his mother's womb, naked shall he return to go as he came, and shall take nothing of his labour, which he may carry away in his hand.

16 And this also is a sore evil, that in all points as he came, so shall he go: and what profit hath he that hath laboured for the wind?

17 All his days also he eateth in darkness, and he hath much sorrow and wrath with his sickness.

18 Behold that which I have seen: it is good and comely

dedit Deus divitias atque substantiam potestatemque ei tribuit ut comedat ex eis et fruatur parte sua et laetetur de labore suo hoc est donum Dei

19. non enim satis recordabitur dierum vitae suae eo quod Deus occupet deliciis cor eius

for one to eat and to drink, and to enjoy the good of all his labour that he taketh under the sun all the days of his life, which God giveth him: for it is his portion.

19 Every man also to whom God hath given riches and wealth, and hath given him power to eat thereof, and to take his portion, and to rejoice in his labour; this is the gift of God.

20 For he shall not much remember the days of his life; because God answereth him in the joy of his heart.

CHAPTER 6

1. est et aliud malum quod vidi sub sole et quidem frequens apud homines

2. vir cui dedit Deus divitias et substantiam et honorem et nihil deest animae eius ex omnibus quae desiderat nec tribuit ei potestatem Deus ut comedat ex eo sed homo extraneus vorabit illud hoc vanitas et magna miseria est

3. si genuerit quispiam

CHAPTER 6

THERE is an evil which I have seen under the sun, and it is common among men:

2 A man to whom God hath given riches, wealth, and honour, so that he wanteth nothing for his soul of all that he desireth, yet God giveth him not power to eat thereof, but a stranger eateth it: this is vanity, and it is an evil disease.

3 If a man beget an hundred children, and live many years, so that the days of his

116

centum et vixerit multos annos et plures dies aetatis habuerit et anima illius non utatur bonis substantiae suae sepulturaque careat de hoc ego pronuntio quod melior illo sit abortivus

4. frustra enim venit et pergit ad tenebras et oblivione delebitur nomen eius

5. non vidit solem neque cognovit distantiam boni et mali

6. etiam si duobus milibus annis vixerit et non fuerit perfruitus bonis nonne ad unum locum properant omnia

7. omnis labor hominis in ore eius sed anima illius non impletur

8. quid habet amplius sapiens ab stulto et quid pauper nisi ut pergat illuc ubi est vita

9. melius est videre quod cupias quam desiderare quod nescias sed et hoc vanitas est et praesumptio spiritus

10. qui futurus est iam vocatum est nomen eius et scitur quod homo sit et non possit contra

years be many, and his soul be not filled with good, and also that he have no burial; I say, that an untimely birth is better than he.

4 For he cometh in with vanity, and departeth in darkness, and his name shall be covered with darkness.

5 Moreover he hath not seen the sun, nor known any thing: this hath more rest than the other.

6 Yea, though he live a thousand years twice told, yet hath he seen no good: do not all go to one place?

7 All the labour of man is for his mouth, and yet the appetite is not filled.

8 For what hath the wise more than the fool? what hath the poor, that knoweth to walk before the living?

9 Better is the sight of the eyes than the wandering of the desire: this is also vanity and vexation of spirit.

10 That which hath been is named already, and it is known that it is man: neither may he contend with him that is mightier than he.

11 Seeing there be many things that increase vanity, what is man the better?

fortiorem se in iudicio contendere

11. verba sunt plurima multa in disputando habentia vanitatem

12 For who knoweth what is good for man in this life, all the days of his vain life which he spendeth as a shadow? for who can tell a man what shall be after him under the sun?

CHAPTER 7

1. quid necesse est homini maiora se quaerere cum ignoret quid conducat sibi in vita sua numero dierum peregrinationis suae et tempore quo velut umbra praeterit aut quis ei poterit indicare quid post eum futurum sub sole sit

2. melius est nomen bonum quam unguenta pretiosa et dies mortis die nativitatis

3. melius est ire ad domum luctus quam ad domum convivii in illa enim finis cunctorum admonetur hominum et vivens cogitat quid futurum sit

4. melior est ira risu quia per tristitiam vultus corrigitur animus delinquentis

CHAPTER 7

A GOOD name is better than precious ointment; and the day of death than the day of one's birth.

2 It is better to go to the house of mourning, than to go to the house of feasting: for that is the end of all men; and the living will lay it to his heart.

3 Sorrow is better than laughter: for by the sadness of the countenance the heart is made better.

4 The heart of the wise is in the house of mourning; but the heart of fools is in the house of mirth.

5 It is better to hear the rebuke of the wise, than for a man to hear the song of fools.

6 For as the crackling of thorns under a pot, so is the laughter of the fool: this also

5. cor sapientium ubi tristitia est et cor stultorum ubi laetitia

6. melius est a sapiente corripi quam stultorum adulatione decipi

7. quia sicut sonitus spinarum ardentium sub olla sic risus stulti sed et hoc vanitas

8. calumnia conturbat sapientem et perdet robur cordis illius

9. melior est finis orationis quam principium melior est patiens arrogante

10. ne velox sis ad irascendum quia ira in sinu stulti requiescit

11. ne dicas quid putas causae est quod priora tempora meliora fuere quam nunc sunt stulta est enim huiuscemodi interrogatio

12. utilior est sapientia cum divitiis et magis prodest videntibus solem

13. sicut enim protegit sapientia sic protegit pecunia hoc autem plus habet eruditio et sapientia quod vitam tribuunt possessori suo

14. considera opera Dei

is vanity.

7 Surely oppression maketh a wise man mad; and a gift destroyeth the heart.

8 Better is the end of a thing than the beginning thereof: and the patient in spirit is better than the proud in spirit.

9 Be not hasty in thy spirit to be angry: for anger resteth in the bosom of fools.

10 Say not thou, What is the cause that the former days were better than these? for thou dost not inquire wisely concerning this.

11 Wisdom is good with an inheritance: and by it there is profit to them that see the sun.

12 For wisdom is a defence, and money is a defence: but the excellency of knowledge is, that wisdom giveth life to them that have it.

13 Consider the work of God: for who can make that straight, which he hath made crooked?

14 In the day of prosperity be joyful, but in the day of adversity consider: God also hath set the one over against the other, to the end that man should find nothing after him.

quod nemo possit corrigere quem ille despexerit

15. in die bona fruere bonis et malam diem praecave sicut enim hanc sic et illam fecit Deus ut non inveniat homo contra eum iustas querimonias

16. haec quoque vidi in diebus vanitatis meae iustus perit in iustitia sua et impius multo vivit tempore in malitia sua

17. noli esse iustus multum neque plus sapias quam necesse est ne obstupescas

18. ne impie agas multum et noli esse stultus ne moriaris in tempore non tuo

19. bonum est te sustentare iustum sed et ab illo ne subtrahas manum tuam quia qui Deum timet nihil neglegit

20. sapientia confortabit sapientem super decem principes civitatis

21. non est enim homo iustus in terra qui faciat bonum et non peccet

22. sed et cunctis sermonibus qui dicuntur ne accommodes cor tuum

15 All things have I seen in the days of my vanity: there is a just man that perisheth in his righteousness, and there is a wicked man that prolongeth his life in his wickedness.

16 Be not righteous over much; neither make thyself over wise: why shouldest thou destroy thyself?

17 Be not over much wicked, neither be thou foolish: why shouldest thou die before thy time?

18 It is good that thou shouldest take hold of this; yea, also from this withdraw not thine hand: for he that feareth God shall come forth of them all.

19 Wisdom strengtheneth the wise more than ten mighty men which are in the city.

20 For there is not a just man upon earth, that doeth good, and sinneth not.

21 Also take no heed unto all words that are spoken; lest thou hear thy servant curse thee:

22 For oftentimes also thine own heart knoweth that thou thyself likewise hast cursed others.

23 All this have I proved by

ne forte audias servum tuum maledicentem tibi

23. scit enim tua conscientia quia et tu crebro maledixisti aliis

24. cuncta temptavi in sapientia dixi sapiens efficiar et ipsa longius recessit a me

25. multo magis quam erat et alta profunditas quis inveniet eam

26. lustravi universa animo meo ut scirem et considerarem et quaererem sapientiam et rationem et ut cognoscerem impietatem stulti et errorem inprudentium

27. et inveni amariorem morte mulierem quae laqueus venatorum est et sagena cor eius vincula sunt manus illius qui placet Deo effugiet eam qui autem peccator est capietur ab illa

28. ecce hoc inveni dicit Ecclesiastes unum et alterum ut invenirem rationem

29. quam adhuc quaerit anima mea et non inveni virum de mille unum repperi mulierem ex

wisdom: I said, I will be wise; but it was far from me.

24 That which is far off, and exceeding deep, who can find it out?

25 I applied mine heart to know, and to search, and to seek out wisdom, and the reason of things, and to know the wickedness of folly, even of foolishness and madness:

26 And I find more bitter than death the woman, whose heart is snares and nets, and her hands as bands: whoso pleaseth God shall escape from her; but the sinner shall be taken by her.

27 Behold, this have I found, saith the preacher, counting one by one, to find out the account:

28 Which yet my soul seeketh, but I find not: one man among a thousand have I found; but a woman among all those have I not found.

29 Lo, this only have I found, that God hath made man upright; but they have sought out many inventions.

omnibus non inveni

30. solummodo hoc inveni quod fecerit Deus hominem rectum et ipse se infinitis miscuerit quaestionibus quis talis ut sapiens est et quis cognovit solutionem verbi

CHAPTER 8

1. sapientia hominis lucet in vultu eius et potentissimus faciem illius commutavit

2. ego os regis observo et praecepta iuramenti Dei

3. ne festines recedere a facie eius neque permaneas in opere malo quia omne quod voluerit faciet

4. et sermo illius potestate plenus est nec dicere ei quisquam potest quare ita facis

5. qui custodit praeceptum non experietur quicquam mali tempus et responsionem cor sapientis intellegit

6. omni negotio tempus est et oportunitas et multa hominis adflictio

CHAPTER 8

WHO is as the wise man? and who knoweth the interpretation of a thing? a man's wisdom maketh his face to shine, and the boldness of his face shall be changed.

2 I counsel thee to keep the king's commandment, and that in regard of the oath of God.

3 Be not hasty to go out of his sight: stand not in an evil thing; for he doeth whatsoever pleaseth him.

4 Where the word of a king is, there is power: and who may say unto him, What doest thou?

5 Whoso keepeth the commandment shall feel no evil thing: and a wise man's heart discerneth both time

7. quia ignorat praeterita et ventura nullo scire potest nuntio

8. non est in hominis dicione prohibere spiritum nec habet potestatem in die mortis nec sinitur quiescere ingruente bello neque salvabit impietas impium

9. omnia haec consideravi et dedi cor meum in cunctis operibus quae fiunt sub sole interdum dominatur homo homini in malum suum

10. vidi impios sepultos qui etiam cum adviverent in loco sancto erant et laudabantur in civitate quasi iustorum operum sed et hoc vanitas est

11. etenim quia non profertur cito contra malos sententia absque ullo timore filii hominum perpetrant mala

12. attamen ex eo quod peccator centies facit malum et per patientiam sustentatur ego cognovi quod erit bonum timentibus Deum qui verentur faciem eius

13. non sit bonum impio nec prolongentur dies

and judgment.

6 Because to every purpose there is time and judgment, therefore the misery of man is great upon him.

7 For he knoweth not that which shall be: for who can tell him when it shall be?

8 There is no man that hath power over the spirit to retain the spirit; neither hath he power in the day of death: and there is no discharge in that war; neither shall wickedness deliver those that are given to it.

9 All this have I seen, and applied my heart unto every work that is done under the sun: there is a time wherein one man ruleth over another to his own hurt.

10 And so I saw the wicked buried, who had come and gone from the place of the holy, and they were forgotten in the city where they had so done: this is also vanity.

11 Because sentence against an evil work is not executed speedily, therefore the heart of the sons of men is fully set in them to do evil.

12 Though a sinner do evil an hundred times, and his days be prolonged, yet surely

eius sed quasi umbra transeant qui non timent faciem Dei

14. est et alia vanitas quae fit super terram sunt iusti quibus multa proveniunt quasi opera egerint impiorum et sunt impii qui ita securi sunt quasi iustorum facta habeant sed et hoc vanissimum iudico

15. laudavi igitur laetitiam quod non esset homini bonum sub sole nisi quod comederet et biberet atque gauderet et hoc solum secum auferret de labore suo in diebus vitae quos dedit ei Deus sub sole

16. et adposui cor meum ut scirem sapientiam et intellegerem distentionem quae versatur in terra est homo qui diebus ac noctibus somnum oculis non capit

17. et intellexi quod omnium operum Dei nullam possit homo invenire rationem eorum quae fiunt sub sole et quanto plus laboraverit ad quaerendum tanto minus inveniat etiam si dixerit

I know that it shall be well with them that fear God, which fear before him:

13 But it shall not be well with the wicked, neither shall he prolong his days, which are as a shadow; because he feareth not before God.

14 There is a vanity which is done upon the earth; that there be just men, unto whom it happeneth according to the work of the wicked; again, there be wicked men, to whom it happeneth according to the work of the righteous: I said that this also is vanity.

15 Then I commended mirth, because a man hath no better thing under the sun, than to eat, and to drink, and to be merry: for that shall abide with him of his labour the days of his life, which God giveth him under the sun.

16 When I applied mine heart to know wisdom, and to see the business that is done upon the earth: (for also there is that neither day nor night seeth sleep with his eyes:)

17 Then I beheld all the work of God, that a man cannot find out the work that is done under the sun: because though a man labour to seek

sapiens se nosse non poterit repperire

it out, yet he shall not find it; yea further; though a wise man think to know it, yet shall he not be able to find it.

CHAPTER 9

CHAPTER 9

1. omnia haec tractavi in corde meo ut curiose intellegerem sunt iusti atque sapientes et opera eorum in manu Dei et tamen nescit homo utrum amore an odio dignus sit
2. sed omnia in futuro servantur incerta eo quod universa aeque eveniant iusto et impio bono et malo mundo et inmundo immolanti victimas et sacrificia contemnenti sicut bonus sic et peccator ut periurus ita et ille qui verum deierat
3. hoc est pessimum inter omnia quae sub sole fiunt quia eadem cunctis eveniunt unde et corda filiorum hominum implentur malitia et contemptu in vita sua et post haec ad inferos deducentur
4. nemo est qui semper vivat et qui huius rei

FOR all this I considered in my heart even to declare all this, that the righteous, and the wise, and their works, are in the hand of God: no man knoweth either love or hatred by all that is before them.

2 All things come alike to all: there is one event to the righteous, and to the wicked; to the good and to the clean, and to the unclean; to him that sacrificeth, and to him that sacrificeth not: as is the good, so is the sinner; and he that sweareth, as he that feareth an oath.

3 This is an evil among all things that are done under the sun, that there is one event unto all: yea, also the heart of the sons of men is full of evil, and madness is in their heart while they live, and after that they go to the dead.

4 For to him that is joined to all the living there is hope: for a living dog is better than

habeat fiduciam melior est canis vivens leone mortuo

5. viventes enim sciunt se esse morituros mortui vero nihil noverunt amplius nec habent ultra mercedem quia oblivioni tradita est memoria eorum

6. amor quoque et odium et invidia simul perierunt nec habent partem in hoc saeculo et in opere quod sub sole geritur

7. vade ergo et comede in laetitia panem tuum et bibe cum gaudio vinum tuum quia Deo placent opera tua

8. omni tempore sint vestimenta tua candida et oleum de capite tuo non deficiat

9. perfruere vita cum uxore quam diligis cunctis diebus vitae instabilitatis tuae qui dati sunt tibi sub sole omni tempore vanitatis tuae haec est enim pars in vita et in labore tuo quod laboras sub sole

10. quodcumque potest manus tua facere instanter operare quia nec

a dead lion.

5 For the living know that they shall die: but the dead know not any thing, neither have they any more a reward; for the memory of them is forgotten.

6 Also their love, and their hatred, and their envy, is now perished; neither have they any more a portion for ever in any thing that is done under the sun.

7 Go thy way, eat thy bread with joy, and drink thy wine with a merry heart; for God now accepteth thy works.

8 Let thy garments be always white; and let thy head lack no ointment.

9 Live joyfully with the wife whom thou lovest all the days of the life of thy vanity, which he hath given thee under the sun, all the days of thy vanity: for that is thy portion in this life, and in thy labour which thou takest under the sun.

10 Whatsoever thy hand findeth to do, do it with thy might; for there is no work, nor device, nor knowledge, nor wisdom, in the grave, whither thou goest.

11 I returned, and saw under

opus nec ratio nec scientia nec sapientia erunt apud inferos quo tu properas

11. verti me alio vidique sub sole nec velocium esse cursum nec fortium bellum nec sapientium panem nec doctorum divitias nec artificum gratiam sed tempus casumque in omnibus

12. nescit homo finem suum sed sicut pisces capiuntur hamo et sicut aves conprehenduntur laqueo sic capiuntur homines tempore malo cum eis extemplo supervenerit

13. hanc quoque vidi sub sole sapientiam et probavi maximam

14. civitas parva et pauci in ea viri venit contra eam rex magnus et vallavit eam extruxitque munitiones per gyrum et perfecta est obsidio

15. inventusque in ea vir pauper et sapiens liberavit urbem per sapientiam suam et nullus deinceps recordatus est hominis illius pauperis

16. et dicebam ego

the sun, that the race is not to the swift, nor the battle to the strong, neither yet bread to the wise, nor yet riches to men of understanding, nor yet favour to men of skill; but time and chance happeneth to them all.

12 For man also knoweth not his time: as the fishes that are taken in an evil net, and as the birds that are caught in the snare; so are the sons of men snared in an evil time, when it falleth suddenly upon them.

13 This wisdom have I seen also under the sun, and it seemed great unto me:

14 There was a little city, and few men within it; and there came a great king against it, and besieged it, and built great bulwarks against it:

15 Now there was found in it a poor wise man, and he by his wisdom delivered the city; yet no man remembered that same poor man.

16 Then said I, Wisdom is better than strength: nevertheless the poor man's wisdom is despised, and his words are not heard.

17 The words of wise men are heard in quiet more than

meliorem esse sapientiam fortitudine quomodo ergo sapientia pauperis contempta est et verba eius non sunt audita

17. verba sapientium audiuntur in silentio plus quam clamor principis inter stultos

18. melior est sapientia quam arma bellica et qui in uno peccaverit multa bona perdet

the cry of him that ruleth among fools.

18 Wisdom is better than weapons of war: but one sinner destroyeth much good.

CHAPTER 10

1. muscae morientes perdunt suavitatem unguenti pretiosior est sapientia et gloria parva ad tempus stultitia

2. cor sapientis in dextera eius et cor stulti in sinistra illius

3. sed et in via stultus ambulans cum ipse insipiens sit omnes stultos aestimat

4. si spiritus potestatem habentis ascenderit super te locum tuum ne dimiseris quia curatio cessare faciet peccata maxima

5. est malum quod vidi

CHAPTER 10

DEAD flies cause the ointment of the apothecary to send forth a stinking savour: so doth a little folly him that is in reputation for wisdom and honour.

2 A wise man's heart is at his right hand; but a fool's heart at his left.

3 Yea also, when he that is a fool walketh by the way, his wisdom faileth him, and he saith to every one that he is a fool.

4 If the spirit of the ruler rise up against thee, leave not thy place; for yielding pacifieth great offences.

5 There is an evil which I

sub sole quasi per errorem egrediens a facie principis

6. positum stultum in dignitate sublimi et divites sedere deorsum

7. vidi servos in equis et principes ambulantes quasi servos super terram

8. qui fodit foveam incidet in eam et qui dissipat sepem mordebit eum coluber

9. qui transfert lapides adfligetur in eis et qui scindit ligna vulnerabitur ab eis

10. si retunsum fuerit ferrum et hoc non ut prius sed hebetatum erit multo labore exacuatur et post industriam sequitur sapientia

11. si mordeat serpens in silentio nihil eo minus habet qui occulte detrahit

12. verba oris sapientis gratia et labia insipientis praecipitabunt eum

13. initium verborum eius stultitia et novissimum oris illius error pessimus

14. stultus verba multiplicat ignorat homo quid ante se fuerit et quod post futurum est quis illi

have seen under the sun, as an error which proceedeth from the ruler:

6 Folly is set in great dignity, and the rich sit in low place.

7 I have seen servants upon horses, and princes walking as servants upon the earth.

8 He that diggeth a pit shall fall into it; and whoso breaketh an hedge, a serpent shall bite him.

9 Whoso removeth stones shall be hurt therewith; and he that cleaveth wood shall be endangered thereby.

10 If the iron be blunt, and he do not whet the edge, then must he put to more strength: but wisdom is profitable to direct.

11 Surely the serpent will bite without enchantment; and a babbler is no better.

12 The words of a wise man's mouth are gracious; but the lips of a fool will swallow up himself.

13 The beginning of the words of his mouth is foolishness: and the end of his talk is mischievous madness.

14 A fool also is full of words: a man cannot tell what shall be; and what shall

poterit indicare

15. labor stultorum adfliget eos qui nesciunt in urbem pergere

16. vae tibi terra cuius rex est puer et cuius principes mane comedunt

17. beata terra cuius rex nobilis est et cuius principes vescuntur in tempore suo ad reficiendum et non ad luxuriam

18. in pigritiis humiliabitur contignatio et in infirmitate manuum perstillabit domus

19. in risu faciunt panem ac vinum ut epulentur viventes et pecuniae oboedient omnia

20. in cogitatione tua regi ne detrahas et in secreto cubiculi tui ne maledixeris diviti quia avis caeli portabit vocem tuam et qui habet pinnas adnuntiabit sententiam

be after him, who can tell him?

15 The labour of the foolish wearieth every one of them, because he knoweth not how to go to the city.

16 Woe to thee, O land, when thy king is a child, and thy princes eat in the morning!

17 Blessed art thou, O land, when thy king is the son of nobles, and thy princes eat in due season, for strength, and not for drunkenness!

18 By much slothfulness the building decayeth; and through idleness of the hands the house droppeth through.

19 A feast is made for laughter, and wine maketh merry: but money answereth all things.

20 Curse not the king, no not in thy thought; and curse not the rich in thy bedchamber: for a bird of the air shall carry the voice, and that which hath wings shall tell the matter.

1. mitte panem tuum super transeuntes aquas quia post multa tempora invenies illum

2. da partem septem necnon et octo quia ignoras quid futurum sit mali super terram

3. si repletae fuerint nubes imbrem super terram effundent si ceciderit lignum ad austrum aut ad aquilonem in quocumque loco ceciderit ibi erit

4. qui observat ventum non seminat et qui considerat nubes numquam metet

5. quomodo ignoras quae sit via spiritus et qua ratione conpingantur ossa in ventre praegnatis sic nescis opera Dei qui fabricator est omnium

6. mane semina sementem tuam et vespere ne cesset manus tua quia nescis quid magis oriatur hoc an illud et si utrumque simul melius erit

7. dulce lumen et

CAST thy bread upon the waters: for thou shalt find it after many days.

2 Give a portion to seven, and also to eight; for thou knowest not what evil shall be upon the earth.

3 If the clouds be full of rain, they empty themselves upon the earth: and if the tree fall toward the south, or toward the north, in the place where the tree falleth, there it shall be.

4 He that observeth the wind shall not sow; and he that regardeth the clouds shall not reap.

5 As thou knowest not what is the way of the spirit, nor how the bones do grow in the womb of her that is with child: even so thou knowest not the works of God who maketh all.

6 In the morning sow thy seed, and in the evening withhold not thine hand: for thou knowest not whether shall prosper, either this or that, or whether they both shall be alike good.

7 Truly the light is sweet,

delectabile est oculis videre solem

and a pleasant thing it is for the eyes to behold the sun:

8. si annis multis vixerit homo et in omnibus his laetatus fuerit meminisse debet tenebrosi temporis et dierum multorum qui cum venerint vanitatis arguentur praeterita

8 But if a man live many years, and rejoice in them all; yet let him remember the days of darkness; for they shall be many. All that cometh is vanity.

9. laetare ergo iuvenis in adulescentia tua et in bono sit cor tuum in diebus iuventutis tuae et ambula in viis cordis tui et in intuitu oculorum tuorum et scito quod pro omnibus his adducet te Deus in iudicium

9 Rejoice, O young man, in thy youth; and let thy heart cheer thee in the days of thy youth, and walk in the ways of thine heart, and in the sight of thine eyes: but know thou, that for all these things God will bring thee into judgment.

10. aufer iram a corde tuo et amove malitiam a carne tua adulescentia enim et voluptas vana sunt

10 Therefore remove sorrow from thy heart, and put away evil from thy flesh: for childhood and youth are vanity.

CHAPTER 12

CHAPTER 12

1. memento creatoris tui in diebus iuventutis tuae antequam veniat tempus adflictionis et adpropinquent anni de quibus dicas non mihi placent

REMEMBER now thy Creator in the days of thy youth, while the evil days come not, nor the years draw nigh, when thou shalt say, I have no pleasure in them;

2. antequam tenebrescat sol et lumen et luna et

2 While the sun, or the light, or the moon, or the stars, be not darkened, nor the clouds

stellae et revertantur
nubes post pluviam
3. quando
commovebuntur custodes
domus et nutabuntur viri
fortissimi et otiosae erunt
molentes inminuto
numero et tenebrescent
videntes per foramina
4. et claudent ostia in
platea in humilitate vocis
molentis et consurgent ad
vocem volucris et
obsurdescent omnes filiae
carminis
5. excelsa quoque
timebunt et formidabunt
in via florebit amigdalum
inpinguabitur lucusta et
dissipabitur capparis
quoniam ibit homo in
domum aeternitatis suae
et circumibunt in platea
plangentes
6. antequam rumpatur
funis argenteus et recurrat
vitta aurea et conteratur
hydria super fontem et
confringatur rota super
cisternam
7. et revertatur pulvis in
terram suam unde erat et
spiritus redeat ad Deum
qui dedit illum
8. vanitas vanitatum dixit
Ecclesiastes omnia

return after the rain:
3 In the day when the
keepers of the house shall
tremble, and the strong men
shall bow themselves, and
the grinders cease because
they are few, and those that
look out of the windows be
darkened,
4 And the doors shall be shut
in the streets, when the sound
of the grinding is low, and he
shall rise up at the voice of
the bird, and all the daughters
of musick shall be brought
low;
5 Also when they shall be
afraid of that which is high,
and fears shall be in the way,
and the almond tree shall
flourish, and the grasshopper
shall be a burden, and desire
shall fail: because man goeth
to his long home, and the
mourners go about the
streets:
6 Or ever the silver cord be
loosed, or the golden bowl be
broken, or the pitcher be
broken at the fountain, or the
wheel broken at the cistern.
7 Then shall the dust return
to the earth as it was: and the
spirit shall return unto God
who gave it.
8 Vanity of vanities, saith

vanitas

9. cumque esset sapientissimus Ecclesiastes docuit populum et enarravit quae fecerit et investigans conposuit parabolas multas

10. quaesivit verba utilia et conscripsit sermones rectissimos ac veritate plenos

11. verba sapientium sicut stimuli et quasi clavi in altum defixi quae per magistrorum concilium data sunt a pastore uno

12. his amplius fili mi ne requiras faciendi plures libros nullus est finis frequensque meditatio carnis adflictio est

13. finem loquendi omnes pariter audiamus Deum time et mandata eius observa hoc est enim omnis homo

14. et cuncta quae fiunt adducet Deus in iudicium pro omni errato sive bonum sive malum sit

the preacher; all is vanity.

9 And moreover, because the preacher was wise, he still taught the people knowledge; yea, he gave good heed, and sought out, and set in order many proverbs.

10 The preacher sought to find out acceptable words: and that which was written was upright, even words of truth.

11 The words of the wise are as goads, and as nails fastened by the masters of assemblies, which are given from one shepherd.

12 And further, by these, my son, be admonished: of making many books there is no end; and much study is a weariness of the flesh.

13 Let us hear the conclusion of the whole matter: Fear God, and keep his commandments: for this is the whole duty of man.

14 For God shall bring every work into judgment, with every secret thing, whether it be good, or whether it be evil.

134

CHAPTER 1

1. osculetur me osculo oris sui quia meliora sunt ubera tua vino
2. fraglantia unguentis optimis oleum effusum nomen tuum ideo adulescentulae dilexerunt te
3. trahe me post te curremus introduxit me rex in cellaria sua exultabimus et laetabimur in te memores uberum tuorum super vinum recti diligunt te
4. nigra sum sed formonsa filiae Hierusalem sicut tabernacula Cedar sicut pelles Salomonis
5. nolite me considerare quod fusca sim quia decoloravit me sol filii matris meae pugnaverunt contra me posuerunt me custodem in vineis vineam meam non custodivi
6. indica mihi quem diligit anima mea ubi pascas ubi cubes in

CHAPTER 1

THE song of songs, which is Solomon's.

2 Let him kiss me with the kisses of his mouth: for thy love is better than wine.

3 Because of the savour of thy good ointments thy name is as ointment poured forth, therefore do the virgins love thee.

4 Draw me, we will run after thee: the king hath brought me into his chambers: we will be glad and rejoice in thee, we will remember thy love more than wine: the upright love thee.

5 I am black, but comely, O ye daughters of Jerusalem, as the tents of Kedar, as the curtains of Solomon.

6 Look not upon me, because I am black, because the sun hath looked upon me: my mother's children were angry with me; they made me the keeper of the vineyards; but mine own vineyard have I not kept.

7 Tell me, O thou whom my soul loveth, where thou

meridie ne vagari incipiam per greges sodalium tuorum

7. si ignoras te o pulchra inter mulieres egredere et abi post vestigia gregum et pasce hedos tuos iuxta tabernacula pastorum

8. equitatui meo in curribus Pharaonis adsimilavi te amica mea

9. pulchrae sunt genae tuae sicut turturis collum tuum sicut monilia

10. murenulas aureas faciemus tibi vermiculatas argento

11. dum esset rex in accubitu suo nardus mea dedit odorem suum

12. fasciculus murrae dilectus meus mihi inter ubera mea commorabitur

13. botrus cypri dilectus meus mihi in vineis Engaddi

14. ecce tu pulchra es amica mea ecce tu pulchra oculi tui columbarum

15. ecce tu pulcher es dilecte mi et decorus lectulus noster floridus

16. tigna domorum nostrarum cedrina laquearia nostra

feedest, where thou makest thy flock to rest at noon: for why should I be as one that turneth aside by the flocks of thy companions?

8 If thou know not, O thou fairest among women, go thy way forth by the footsteps of the flock, and feed thy kids beside the shepherds' tents.

9 I have compared thee, O my love, to a company of horses in Pharaoh's chariots.

10 Thy cheeks are comely with rows of jewels, thy neck with chains of gold.

11 We will make thee borders of gold with studs of silver.

12 While the king sitteth at his table, my spikenard sendeth forth the smell thereof.

13 A bundle of myrrh is my wellbeloved unto me; he shall lie all night betwixt my breasts.

14 My beloved is unto me as a cluster of camphire in the vineyards of En-gedi.

15 Behold, thou art fair, my love; behold, thou art fair; thou hast doves' eyes.

16 Behold, thou art fair, my beloved, yea, pleasant: also our bed is green.

cypressina

17 The beams of our house are cedar, and our rafters of fir.

CHAPTER 2

CHAPTER 2

1. ego flos campi et lilium convallium
2. sicut lilium inter spinas sic amica mea inter filias
3. sicut malum inter ligna silvarum sic dilectus meus inter filios sub umbra illius quam desideraveram sedi et fructus eius dulcis gutturi meo
4. introduxit me in cellam vinariam ordinavit in me caritatem
5. fulcite me floribus stipate me malis quia amore langueo
6. leva eius sub capite meo et dextera illius amplexabitur me
7. adiuro vos filiae Hierusalem per capreas cervosque camporum ne suscitetis neque evigilare faciatis dilectam quoadusque ipsa velit
8. vox dilecti mei ecce iste venit saliens in montibus transiliens

I AM the rose of Sharon, and the lily of the valleys.

2 As the lily among thorns, so is my love among the daughters.

3 As the apple tree among the trees of the wood, so is my beloved among the sons. I sat down under his shadow with great delight, and his fruit was sweet to my taste.

4 He brought me to the banqueting house, and his banner over me was love.

5 Stay me with flagons, comfort me with apples: for I am sick of love.

6 His left hand is under my head, and his right hand doth embrace me.

7 I charge you, O ye daughters of Jerusalem, by the roes, and by the hinds of the field, that ye stir not up, nor awake my love, till he please.

8 The voice of my beloved! behold, he cometh leaping upon the mountains, skipping

colles

9. similis est dilectus meus capreae hinuloque cervorum en ipse stat post parietem nostrum despiciens per fenestras prospiciens per cancellos

10. et dilectus meus loquitur mihi surge propera amica mea formonsa mea et veni

11. iam enim hiemps transiit imber abiit et recessit

12. flores apparuerunt in terra tempus putationis advenit vox turturis audita est in terra nostra

13. ficus protulit grossos suos vineae florent dederunt odorem surge amica mea speciosa mea et veni

14. columba mea in foraminibus petrae in caverna maceriae ostende mihi faciem tuam sonet vox tua in auribus meis vox enim tua dulcis et facies tua decora

15. capite nobis vulpes vulpes parvulas quae demoliuntur vineas nam vinea nostra floruit

16. dilectus meus mihi et ego illi qui pascitur inter

upon the hills.

9 My beloved is like a roe or a young hart: behold, he standeth behind our wall, he looketh forth at the windows, shewing himself through the lattice.

10 My beloved spake, and said unto me, Rise up, my love, my fair one, and come away.

11 For, lo, the winter is past, the rain is over and gone;

12 The flowers appear on the earth; the time of the singing of birds is come, and the voice of the turtle is heard in our land;

13 The fig tree putteth forth her green figs, and the vines with the tender grape give a good smell. Arise, my love, my fair one, and come away.

14 O my dove, that art in the clefts of the rock, in the secret places of the stairs, let me see thy countenance, let me hear thy voice; for sweet is thy voice, and thy countenance is comely.

15 Take us the foxes, the little foxes, that spoil the vines: for our vines have tender grapes.

16 My beloved is mine, and I am his: he feedeth among

lilia

17. donec adspiret dies et inclinentur umbrae revertere similis esto dilecte mi capreae aut hinulo cervorum super montes Bether

the lilies.

17 Until the day break, and the shadows flee away, turn, my beloved, and be thou like a roe or a young hart upon the mountains of Bether.

CHAPTER 3

1. in lectulo meo per noctes quaesivi quem diligit anima mea quaesivi illum et non inveni

2. surgam et circuibo civitatem per vicos et plateas quaeram quem diligit anima mea quaesivi illum et non inveni

3. invenerunt me vigiles qui custodiunt civitatem num quem dilexit anima mea vidistis

4. paululum cum pertransissem eos inveni quem diligit anima mea tenui eum nec dimittam donec introducam illum in domum matris meae et in cubiculum genetricis meae

5. adiuro vos filiae Hierusalem per capreas

CHAPTER 3

BY night on my bed I sought him whom my soul loveth: I sought him, but I found him not.

2 I will rise now, and go about the city in the streets, and in the broad ways I will seek him whom my soul loveth: I sought him, but I found him not.

3 The watchmen that go about the city found me: to whom I said, Saw ye him whom my soul loveth?

4 It was but a little that I passed from them, but I found him whom my soul loveth: I held him, and would not let him go, until I had brought him into my mother's house, and into the chamber of her that conceived me.

5 I charge you, O ye daughters of Jerusalem, by

cervosque camporum ne suscitetis neque evigilare faciatis dilectam donec ipsa velit

6. quae est ista quae ascendit per desertum sicut virgula fumi ex aromatibus murrae et turis et universi pulveris pigmentarii

7. en lectulum Salomonis sexaginta fortes ambiunt ex fortissimis Israhel

8. omnes tenentes gladios et ad bella doctissimi uniuscuiusque ensis super femur suum propter timores nocturnos

9. ferculum fecit sibi rex Salomon de lignis Libani

10. columnas eius fecit argenteas reclinatorium aureum ascensum purpureum media caritate constravit propter filias Hierusalem

11. egredimini et videte filiae Sion regem Salomonem in diademate quo coronavit eum mater sua in die disposionis illius et in die laetitiae cordis eius

the roes, and by the hinds of the field, that ye stir not up, nor awake my love, till he please.

6 Who is this that cometh out of the wilderness like pillars of smoke, perfumed with myrrh and frankincense, with all powders of the merchant?

7 Behold his bed, which is Solomon's; threescore valiant men are about it, of the valiant of Israel.

8 They all hold swords, being expert in war: every man hath his sword upon his thigh because of fear in the night.

9 King Solomon made himself a chariot of the wood of Lebanon.

10 He made the pillars thereof of silver, the bottom thereof of gold, the covering of it of purple, the midst thereof being paved with love, for the daughters of Jerusalem.

11 Go forth, O ye daughters of Zion, and behold king Solomon with the crown wherewith his mother crowned him in the day of his espousals, and in the day of the gladness of his heart.

CHAPTER 4

1. quam pulchra es amica mea quam pulchra es oculi tui columbarum absque eo quod intrinsecus latet capilli tui sicut greges caprarum quae ascenderunt de monte Galaad

2. dentes tui sicut greges tonsarum quae ascenderunt de lavacro omnes gemellis fetibus et sterilis non est inter eas

3. sicut vitta coccinea labia tua et eloquium tuum dulce sicut fragmen mali punici ita genae tuae absque eo quod intrinsecus latet

4. sicut turris David collum tuum quae aedificata est cum propugnaculis mille clypei pendent ex ea omnis armatura fortium

5. duo ubera tua sicut duo hinuli capreae gemelli qui pascuntur in liliis

6. donec adspiret dies et inclinentur umbrae vadam ad montem murrae et ad collem turis

7. tota pulchra es amica

BEHOLD, thou art fair, my love; behold, thou art fair; thou hast doves' eyes within thy locks: thy hair is as a flock of goats, that appear from mount Gilead.

2 Thy teeth are like a flock of sheep that are even shorn, which came up from the washing; whereof every one bear twins, and none is barren among them.

3 Thy lips are like a thread of scarlet, and thy speech is comely: thy temples are like a piece of a pomegranate within thy locks.

4 Thy neck is like the tower of David builded for an armoury, whereon there hang a thousand bucklers, all shields of mighty men.

5 Thy two breasts are like two young roes that are twins, which feed among the lilies.

6 Until the day break, and the shadows flee away, I will get me to the mountain of myrrh, and to the hill of frankincense.

7 Thou art all fair, my love; there is no spot in thee.

mea et macula non est in te

8. veni de Libano sponsa veni de Libano veni coronaberis de capite Amana de vertice Sanir et Hermon de cubilibus leonum de montibus pardorum

9. vulnerasti cor meum soror mea sponsa vulnerasti cor meum in uno oculorum tuorum et in uno crine colli tui

10. quam pulchrae sunt mammae tuae soror mea sponsa pulchriora ubera tua vino et odor unguentorum tuorum super omnia aromata

11. favus distillans labia tua sponsa mel et lac sub lingua tua et odor vestimentorum tuorum sicut odor turis

12. hortus conclusus soror mea sponsa hortus conclusus fons signatus

13. emissiones tuae paradisus malorum punicorum cum pomorum fructibus cypri cum nardo

14. nardus et crocus fistula et cinnamomum cum universis lignis Libani murra et aloe cum

8 Come with me from Lebanon, my spouse, with me from Lebanon: look from the top of Amana, from the top of Shenir and Hermon, from the lions' dens, from the mountains of the leopards.

9 Thou hast ravished my heart, my sister, my spouse; thou hast ravished my heart with one of thine eyes, with one chain of thy neck.

10 How fair is thy love, my sister, my spouse! how much better is thy love than wine! and the smell of thine ointments than all spices!

11 Thy lips, O my spouse, drop as the honeycomb: honey and milk are under thy tongue; and the smell of thy garments is like the smell of Lebanon.

12 A garden inclosed is my sister, my spouse; a spring shut up, a fountain sealed.

13 Thy plants are an orchard of pomegranates, with pleasant fruits; camphire, with spikenard,

14 Spikenard and saffron; calamus and cinnamon, with all trees of frankincense; myrrh and aloes, with all the chief spices:

omnibus primis unguentis
15. fons hortorum puteus aquarum viventium quae fluunt impetu de Libano
16. surge aquilo et veni auster perfla hortum meum et fluant aromata illius

15 A fountain of gardens, a well of living waters, and streams from Lebanon.

16 Awake, O north wind; and come, thou south; blow upon my garden, that the spices thereof may flow out. Let my beloved come into his garden, and eat his pleasant fruits.

CHAPTER 5

1. veniat dilectus meus in hortum suum et comedat fructum pomorum suorum veni in hortum meum soror mea sponsa messui murram meam cum aromatibus meis comedi favum cum melle meo bibi vinum meum cum lacte meo comedite amici bibite et inebriamini carissimi

2. ego dormio et cor meum vigilat vox dilecti mei pulsantis aperi mihi soror mea amica mea columba mea inmaculata mea quia caput meum plenum est rore et cincinni mei guttis noctium

3. expoliavi me tunica

CHAPTER 5

I AM come into my garden, my sister, my spouse: I have gathered my myrrh with my spice; I have eaten my honeycomb with my honey; I have drunk my wine with my milk: eat, O friends; drink, yea, drink abundantly, O beloved.

2 I sleep, but my heart waketh: it is the voice of my beloved that knocketh, saying, Open to me, my sister, my love, my dove, my undefiled: for my head is filled with dew, and my locks with the drops of the night.

3 I have put off my coat; how shall I put it on? I have washed my feet; how shall I defile them?

4 My beloved put in his hand

mea quomodo induar illa lavi pedes meos quomodo inquinabo illos

4. dilectus meus misit manum suam per foramen et venter meus intremuit ad tactum eius

5. surrexi ut aperirem dilecto meo manus meae stillaverunt murra digiti mei pleni murra probatissima

6. pessulum ostii aperui dilecto meo at ille declinaverat atque transierat anima mea liquefacta est ut locutus est quaesivi et non inveni illum vocavi et non respondit mihi

7. invenerunt me custodes qui circumeunt civitatem percusserunt me vulneraverunt me tulerunt pallium meum mihi custodes murorum

8. adiuro vos filiae Hierusalem si inveneritis dilectum meum ut nuntietis ei quia amore langueo

9. qualis est dilectus tuus ex dilecto o pulcherrima mulierum qualis est dilectus tuus ex dilecto quia sic adiurasti nos

by the hole of the door, and my bowels were moved for him.

5 I rose up to open to my beloved; and my hands dropped with myrrh, and my fingers with sweet smelling myrrh, upon the handles of the lock.

6 I opened to my beloved; but my beloved had withdrawn himself, and was gone: my soul failed when he spake: I sought him, but I could not find him; I called him, but he gave me no answer.

7 The watchmen that went about the city found me, they smote me, they wounded me; the keepers of the walls took away my veil from me.

8 I charge you, O daughters of Jerusalem, if ye find my beloved, that ye tell him, that I am sick of love.

9 What is thy beloved more than another beloved, O thou fairest among women? what is thy beloved more than another beloved, that thou dost so charge us?

10 My beloved is white and ruddy, the chiefest among ten thousand.

11 His head is as the most

10. dilectus meus candidus et rubicundus electus ex milibus

11. caput eius aurum optimum comae eius sicut elatae palmarum nigrae quasi corvus

12. oculi eius sicut columbae super rivulos aquarum quae lacte sunt lotae et resident iuxta fluenta plenissima

13. genae illius sicut areolae aromatum consitae a pigmentariis labia eius lilia distillantia murram primam

14. manus illius tornatiles aureae plenae hyacinthis venter eius eburneus distinctus sapphyris

15. crura illius columnae marmoreae quae fundatae sunt super bases aureas species eius ut Libani electus ut cedri

16. guttur illius suavissimum et totus desiderabilis talis est dilectus meus et iste est amicus meus filiae Hierusalem

17. quo abiit dilectus tuus o pulcherrima mulierum quo declinavit dilectus tuus et quaeremus eum

fine gold, his locks are bushy, and black as a raven.

12 His eyes are as the eyes of doves by the rivers of waters, washed with milk, and fitly set.

13 His cheeks are as a bed of spices, as sweet flowers: his lips like lilies, dropping sweet smelling myrrh.

14 His hands are as gold rings set with the beryl: his belly is as bright ivory overlaid with sapphires.

15 His legs are as pillars of marble, set upon sockets of fine gold: his countenance is as Lebanon, excellent as the cedars.

16 His mouth is most sweet: yea, he is altogether lovely. This is my beloved, and this is my friend, O daughters of Jerusalem.

CHAPTER 6

1. dilectus meus descendit in hortum suum ad areolam aromatis ut pascatur in hortis et lilia colligat

2. ego dilecto meo et dilectus meus mihi qui pascitur inter lilia

3. pulchra es amica mea suavis et decora sicut Hierusalem terribilis ut castrorum acies ordinata

4. averte oculos tuos a me quia ipsi me avolare fecerunt capilli tui sicut grex caprarum quae apparuerunt de Galaad

5. dentes tui sicut grex ovium quae ascenderunt de lavacro omnes gemellis fetibus et sterilis non est in eis

6. sicut cortex mali punici genae tuae absque occultis tuis

7. sexaginta sunt reginae et octoginta concubinae et adulescentularum non est numerus

8. una est columba mea perfecta mea una est

CHAPTER 6

WHITHER is thy beloved gone, O thou fairest among women? whither is thy beloved turned aside? that we may seek him with thee.

2 My beloved is gone down into his garden, to the beds of spices, to feed in the gardens, and to gather lilies.

3 I am my beloved's, and my beloved is mine: he feedeth among the lilies.

4 Thou art beautiful, O my love, as Tirzah, comely as Jerusalem, terrible as an army with banners.

5 Turn away thine eyes from me, for they have overcome me: thy hair is as a flock of goats that appear from Gilead.

6 Thy teeth are as a flock of sheep which go up from the washing, whereof every one beareth twins, and there is not one barren among them.

7 As a piece of a pomegranate are thy temples within thy locks.

8 There are threescore queens, and fourscore

matris suae electa genetrici suae viderunt illam filiae et beatissimam praedicaverunt reginae et concubinae et laudaverunt eam

9. quae est ista quae progreditur quasi aurora consurgens pulchra ut luna electa ut sol terribilis ut acies ordinata

10. descendi ad hortum nucum ut viderem poma convallis ut inspicerem si floruisset vinea et germinassent mala punica

11. nescivi anima mea conturbavit me propter quadrigas Aminadab

12. revertere revertere Sulamitis revertere revertere ut intueamur te

concubines, and virgins without number.

9 My dove, my undefiled is but one; she is the only one of her mother, she is the choice one of her that bare her. The daughters saw her, and blessed her; yea, the queens and the concubines, and they praised her.

10 Who is she that looketh forth as the morning, fair as the moon, clear as the sun, and terrible as an army with banners?

11 I went down into the garden of nuts to see the fruits of the valley, and to see whether the vine flourished, and the pomegranates budded.

12 Or ever I was aware, my soul made me like the chariots of Amminadib.

13 Return, return, O Shulamite; return, return, that we may look upon thee. What will ye see in the Shulamite? As it were the company of two armies.

CHAPTER 7

1. quid videbis in Sulamiten nisi choros

CHAPTER 7

HOW beautiful are thy feet with shoes, O prince's

castrorum quam pulchri sunt gressus tui in calciamentis filia principis iunctura feminum tuorum sicut monilia quae fabricata sunt manu artificis

2. umbilicus tuus crater tornatilis numquam indigens poculis venter tuus sicut acervus tritici vallatus liliis

3. duo ubera tua sicut duo hinuli gemelli capreae

4. collum tuum sicut turris eburnea oculi tui sicut piscinae in Esebon quae sunt in porta filiae multitudinis nasus tuus sicut turris Libani quae respicit contra Damascum

5. caput tuum ut Carmelus et comae capitis tui sicut purpura regis vincta canalibus

6. quam pulchra es et quam decora carissima in deliciis

7. statura tua adsimilata est palmae et ubera tua botris

8. dixi ascendam in palmam adprehendam fructus eius et erunt ubera tua sicut botri vineae et odor oris tui sicut

daughter! the joints of thy thighs are like jewels, the work of the hands of a cunning workman.

2 Thy navel is like a round goblet, which wanteth not liquor: thy belly is like an heap of wheat set about with lilies.

3 Thy two breasts are like two young roes that are twins.

4 Thy neck is as a tower of ivory; thine eyes like the fishpools in Heshbon, by the gate of Bath-rabbim: thy nose is as the tower of Lebanon which looketh toward Damascus.

5 Thine head upon thee is like Carmel, and the hair of thine head like purple; the king is held in the galleries.

6 How fair and how pleasant art thou, O love, for delights!

7 This thy stature is like to a palm tree, and thy breasts to clusters of grapes.

8 I said, I will go up to the palm tree, I will take hold of the boughs thereof: now also thy breasts shall be as clusters of the vine, and the smell of thy nose like apples;

9 And the roof of thy mouth like the best wine for my

149

malorum

9. guttur tuum sicut vinum optimum dignum dilecto meo ad potandum labiisque et dentibus illius ruminandum

10. ego dilecto meo et ad me conversio eius

11. veni dilecte mi egrediamur in agrum commoremur in villis

12. mane surgamus ad vineas videamus si floruit vinea si flores fructus parturiunt si floruerunt mala punica ibi dabo tibi ubera mea

13. mandragorae dederunt odorem in portis nostris omnia poma nova et vetera dilecte mi servavi tibi

beloved, that goeth down sweetly, causing the lips of those that are asleep to speak.

10 I am my beloved's, and his desire is toward me.

11 Come, my beloved, let us go forth into the field; let us lodge in the villages.

12 Let us get up early to the vineyards; let us see if the vine flourish, whether the tender grape appear, and the pomegranates bud forth: there will I give thee my loves.

13 The mandrakes give a smell, and at our gates are all manner of pleasant fruits, new and old, which I have laid up for thee, O my beloved.

CHAPTER 8

1. quis mihi det te fratrem meum sugentem ubera matris meae ut inveniam te foris et deosculer et iam me nemo despiciat

2. adprehendam te et ducam in domum matris meae ibi me docebis et dabo tibi poculum ex vino condito et mustum

CHAPTER 8

O THAT thou wert as my brother, that sucked the breasts of my mother! when I should find thee without, I would kiss thee; yea, I should not be despised.

2 I would lead thee, and bring thee into my mother's house, who would instruct me: I would cause thee to

malorum granatorum meorum

3. leva eius sub capite meo et dextera illius amplexabitur me

4. adiuro vos filiae Hierusalem ne suscitetis et evigilare faciatis dilectam donec ipsa velit

5. quae est ista quae ascendit de deserto deliciis affluens et nixa super dilectum suum sub arbore malo suscitavi te ibi corrupta est mater tua ibi violata est genetrix tua

6. pone me ut signaculum super cor tuum ut signaculum super brachium tuum quia fortis est ut mors dilectio dura sicut inferus aemulatio lampades eius lampades ignis atque flammarum

7. aquae multae non poterunt extinguere caritatem nec flumina obruent illam si dederit homo omnem substantiam domus suae pro dilectione quasi nihil despicient eum

8. soror nostra parva et ubera non habet quid faciemus sorori nostrae in die quando adloquenda

drink of spiced wine of the juice of my pomegranate.

3 His left hand should be under my head, and his right hand should embrace me.

4 I charge you, O daughters of Jerusalem, that ye stir not up, nor awake my love, until he please.

5 Who is this that cometh up from the wilderness, leaning upon her beloved? I raised thee up under the apple tree: there thy mother brought thee forth: there she brought thee forth that bare thee.

6 Set me as a seal upon thine heart, as a seal upon thine arm: for love is strong as death; jealousy is cruel as the grave: the coals thereof are coals of fire, which hath a most vehement flame.

7 Many waters cannot quench love, neither can the floods drown it: if a man would give all the substance of his house for love, it would utterly be contemned.

8 We have a little sister, and she hath no breasts: what shall we do for our sister in the day when she shall be spoken for?

9 If she be a wall, we will build upon her a palace of

est

9. si murus est aedificemus super eum propugnacula argentea si ostium est conpingamus illud tabulis cedrinis

10. ego murus et ubera mea sicut turris ex quo facta sum coram eo quasi pacem repperiens

11. vinea fuit Pacifico in ea quae habet populos tradidit eam custodibus vir adfert pro fructu eius mille argenteos

12. vinea mea coram me est mille tui Pacifice et ducenti his qui custodiunt fructus eius

13. quae habitas in hortis amici auscultant fac me audire vocem tuam

14. fuge dilecte mi et adsimilare capreae hinuloque cervorum super montes aromatum

silver: and if she be a door, we will inclose her with boards of cedar.

10 I am a wall, and my breasts like towers: then was I in his eyes as one that found favour.

11 Solomon had a vineyard at Baal-hamon; he let out the vineyard unto keepers; every one for the fruit thereof was to bring a thousand pieces of silver.

12 My vineyard, which is mine, is before me: thou, O Solomon, must have a thousand, and those that keep the fruit thereof two hundred.

13 Thou that dwellest in the gardens, the companions hearken to thy voice: cause me to hear it.

14 Make haste, my beloved, and be thou like to a roe or to a young hart upon the mountains of spices.

61043709R00086